SUPER EASY ORGANIC LOW CARB DIET FOR BEGINNERS

Your Weight Loss Revolution with Eco-Friendly Choices and Nutritional Excellences | 1200 Days of Quick and Tasty Recipes for Your Everyday Wellbeing

FABIO FERRALDESCHI

D1519092

Table of Contents

A Special Gift for My Readers

Thank you for choosing "Super Easy Organic Low Carb Diet for Beginners." As you embark on this new path towards health and wellness with a focus on low-carb organic eating, I am honored to be part of your transformative journey.

To express my gratitude for your commitment to bettering your health, I am thrilled to offer you a special gift. Delve deeper into the essence of healthy, sustainable living with a bonus text entitled "Organic Farming - A Journey from Soil to Table." This bonus material is designed to enhance your understanding of the core principles of organic farming, enriched by insights and personal experiences I've gathered along the way.

To access your bonus, simply scan the QR code provided below. This is my way of saying thank you and to further support your commitment to a healthy, organic, low-carb lifestyle.

May your journey towards health and simplicity in eating be as fulfilling as it is nourishing.

Dear Reader,

Welcome to "Super Easy Organic Low Carb Diet for Beginners." This book is your gateway to understanding how an organic, low-carb diet can be a game-changer for your health and well-being.

The insights and recommendations you will find here are born from extensive research and hands-on experience in the realm of organic nutrition and low-carbohydrate living. Through my journey, I have learned the critical role that the right food choices play in maintaining vitality and health, particularly the power of a low-carb approach to eating.

As you delve into the pages of this book, please consider it as a guide on your path to wellness, but not as a stand-in for tailored medical advice. It's important to consult with a nutritionist or healthcare professional to ensure that the low-carb lifestyle adjustments you make are well-suited to your personal health requirements.

This book is crafted for those ready to adopt an organic, low-carb diet, paying close attention to beginners who may be navigating this lifestyle for the first time. Should you wish to leverage the information for business or commercial ventures, I advise caution and recommend seeking further expertise and detailed counsel.

Remember, each person's journey to health is personal and distinct. The natural world provides a bounty of choices, and by honoring and listening to our bodies, we can select the most nourishing paths.

I trust that "Super Easy Organic Low Carb Diet for Beginners" will illuminate and motivate you as you start on your road to a more healthful, organic way of life, complemented by the guidance of a knowledgeable nutritionist.

With respect and warmth,

Fabio Ferraldeschi

Introduction

Losing weight is a journey that requires commitment, discipline, and a nourishing fuel source. For many, this journey is walking a fine line between deprivation and indulgence, struggling to find balance amidst confusing diet trends and mixed health messages. Increasingly, people are beginning to understand that what we eat is as important as how much we eat and that real, sustainable change happens by listening to our bodies and empowering our well-being from within.

This book aims to walk with you along the path of your own transformation, equipping you with simple principles and practices that support lasting weight loss from the inside out. Rather than dictate a restricted set of rules, it offers guidance to help you tune into your unique needs and find fulfilling harmony. At the core is a fusion of two conceptually aligned frameworks - organic whole foods and low-carb eating. Organic nutrition embraces nature's garden as the most wholesome pharmacy. Organic fruits and vegetables, nuts, seeds, legumes and beans are overflowing with fiber, vitamins, minerals and protective plant compounds. Choosing organic supports not only personal health but also environmental and social well-being. Organic agriculture is gentler on the earth and on the farmers who provide for us. It benefits our soil, waters and wildlife, all critical parts of a sustainable model. Organic foods are raised without toxic pesticides, synthetic fertilizers or GMOs, allowing their innate goodness to shine through in a pure, chemical-free form.

Consuming organic whole foods automatically incorporates low-carb principles, as nutrient-dense plants are naturally low in starchy carbs. A low-carb strategy has been shown to be beneficial for controlling weight because it stabilizes insulin and blood sugar levels. Without the spikes and crashes caused by refined carbs and added sugars, appetite regulation improves, and fat burning is supported. At the same time, incorporating organic produce ensures you receive broad nourishment instead of restrictive deprivation. Low-carb eating doesn't necessitate "no carb" - it simply shifts focus to quality whole-food carbs from organic fruits, non-starchy vegetables, nuts and seeds.

Individually, the research backing organic and low-carb diets is compelling. But their combined power promises even greater transformation, physically and mentally. Weight loss becomes attainable through gentle, sustainable means - nourishing your body with the very best fuel while updating your lifestyle, not depriving it. And by choosing organic, you care for your well-being as holistically as possible, down to the cellular level, with rewarding ripple effects in your community and environment, too.

This book breaks new ground by uniting these two synergistic frameworks into an integrated whole-food lifestyle approach. Each chapter unveils practical and inspirational insights to guide your evolving journey. You'll discover how to stock your organic pantry and plan satisfying meals, how to fine-tune your carb intake in a flexible yet effective manner, and tips to stay motivated along the way. Case studies from people who have experienced profound renewal share their lessons learned.

You'll find space to consider your own relationship with food and the deeper messages your body is trying to convey, in addition to the objective science. Losing weight sustainably is about more than shedding pounds - it's about nurturing wellness from the inside out and cultivating self-care practices that last a lifetime. By weaving together organic choices and an easily customizable low-carb approach, this book empowers you to fulfill your health goals compassionately.

Whether it's 5 or 50 pounds you seek to set free, this customized organic low-carb path gets to the root of weighty issues and guides you back into balance from a full-body, holistic perspective. You'll discover how attuning to your body's natural signals can lead to balanced energy, stable moods, and the agility to ride life's waves gracefully - while also reaching and maintaining a healthy weight. Each step invites deeper care for yourself and a reverence for the incredible natural systems that sustain us all on our shared planet. By walking in harmony with Earth's ecological rhythms, your renewal ripples outwards to awaken wellness in the community and environment, too.

There's such resilience within us all, just waiting to blossom when given the proper nurturance. This book holds space for you to walk your unique journey with openness, acceptance and compassion - for yourself and for all. Its integrated organic low-carb approach respects your body as a holistic, ever-evolving system and invites renewal at a deep cellular level through foods that heal and uplift. Each chapter provides guidance yet honors that your path is yours alone to tread.

In the end, changing our connection with food and fitness is an act of self-love. By committing to nourishing yourself with organic whole foods in a balanced, low-carb manner, incredible renewal is possible. Weight loss results from gentler inner alignment, not deprivation or willpower. Deeper still, you cultivate self-care practices and a reverence for nature that overflows into joyful, sustainable living.

Whether you seek to release 5 or 50 pounds, this integrated organic low-carb path lights the way. Commit to walking it with patience, care and, an open heart, and lasting transformation at all levels - physical, mental and spiritual - awaits you. Your journey begins here, friend. Let's marvel together at all you have to discover along the way.

Chapter 1
Low Carb for Weight Loss

Why Low Carb Works for Shedding Pounds

Low carbohydrate diets have become widely popular for their ability to help people lose weight and keep it off long term. When trying to lose weight, reducing carbohydrate intake is one of the most effective strategies, as carbs have a significant impact on the body's metabolism and fat storage mechanisms. The primary reason low-carb diets are so successful for weight loss comes down to how carbohydrates affect blood sugar and insulin levels. When carbohydrate-rich foods like bread, pasta, cereals and starchy vegetables are consumed, they are quickly broken down into glucose, which causes blood sugar levels to rise sharply. In order to process all this glucose and bring blood sugar back to normal levels, the pancreas secretes the hormone insulin into the bloodstream. Insulin's main role is to transport glucose from the bloodstream into the body's cells, where it can either be used immediately for energy needs or stored away as fat for future use.

On the other hand, if more carbohydrates are ingested than the body needs for immediate energy, the extra glucose cannot be utilized and needs to be changed to and turned into body fat by a procedure known as fresh lipogenesis. When blood sugar rises rapidly after eating carbs, it triggers a large insulin response from the pancreas on a frequent, ongoing basis. This constant shuttling of glucose into fat cells via insulin contributes significantly to weight gain over time. Additionally, the sharp spikes in blood glucose that occur after carb consumption signal to the brain that more food is needed very soon to maintain optimal energy levels. As a result, the hunger hormones ghrelin and grehlin remain elevated, making the dieter feel hungrier more often and have more cravings for calorie-dense carbohydrate-rich snack foods. This perpetuates a cycle of overeating and further weight gain if not addressed. On the other hand, by limiting carbohydrate intake and focusing on protein, fat and low-starch vegetables, consumption of low-carb diets prevents these frequent insulin spikes and subsequent fat storage while stabilizing blood sugar levels. Low-carb diets also help control appetite by minimizing hunger hormone fluctuations, so dieters feel more satisfied for longer periods on fewer calories.

With less glucose available from dietary carbs to store as fat, the body is forced instead to tap into existing fat cells through a process known as lipolysis, essentially burning fat for fuel. In this fat-burning state, the liver produces ketones from fat to supply energy to the tissues rather than relying on carbohydrates. Studies back up the premise that following a low-carb eating pattern leads to better weight loss outcomes overall compared to reducing fat or calories alone due to its direct impact on altering insulin sensitivity and metabolic function in a way that promotes fat burning over storage. The science supports that the mechanisms of reduced carbohydrate intake are key to understanding how and why these diets support weight control.

How Low Carb Diets Promote Weight Loss?

The Role of Insulin in Fat Storage

When carbohydrates from foods like grains, starchy vegetables and sugars are consumed, they rapidly raise blood glucose levels. This causes the pancreas to release the insulin hormone. The main job of insulin is to move glucose from the bloodstream into cells, which lowers blood sugar levels. If insulin levels aren't lowered soon after, this excess glucose is converted to and stored as body fat through a process called de novo lipogenesis. However, after a high-carb meal, there is often excess glucose circulating beyond what cells need immediately for energy. This extra glucose is transformed into and stored as body fat through a process known as de novo lipogenesis if insulin levels aren't decreased shortly after.

Persistently high insulin from frequent carb intake promotes ongoing fat storage over time.

Enabling Fat Burning through Low Insulin

In contrast, low-carb diets modulate insulin secretion and sensitivity. With fewer carbs consumed, blood sugar and insulin spikes are lower and less frequent. This allows hormones like glucagon to work more effectively. Glucagon stimulates gluconeogenesis, generating glucose from proteins to maintain energy levels, as well as lipolysis - the breakdown of fatty acids from fat cells.

When insulin levels are kept low for an extended period, the body learns to burn fatty acids and ketones via ketosis rather than relying on glucose. Fat mobilization from adipose tissue provides fuel, supporting sustained energy without additional fat storage. Over time, metabolic fat-adaptation occurs on low carb.

Reducing Hunger through Stable Blood Sugar

Low-carb eating also aids weight loss by controlling appetite. Constant blood sugar spikes and drops cause hunger hormones like ghrelin to fluctuate wildly, triggering more frequent feelings of hunger and carb cravings.

However, low-carb diets stabilize blood glucose and moderate insulin so hunger hormone levels remain balanced. Coupled with choosing satiating proteins and fats, low carbers feel fuller for longer and consume fewer daily calories naturally - crucial for weight loss success.

The Science Behind Carbs and Fat Storage

Low-carb diets have received criticism over the years for supposedly being unhealthy or ineffective because of a long-held belief that all calories are equal and diet composition does not matter for weight management. However, extensive research indicates that the macronutrient quality and timing of calories absolutely influence the body's fat-storing versus fat-burning pathways. Some of the scientific evidence to support low-carb methods includes data showing that reducing carb intake leads to significant weight loss even without calorie counting.

In various clinical trials, study participants assigned to low-carb groups lost, on average, over two times more weight after 6 months compared to low-fat dieters despite eating the same or greater number of calories. Other studies show that low-carb diets increase levels of the fat-regulating hormone leptin and decrease levels of the hunger hormone ghrelin compared to calorie-restricted, carbohydrate-focused diets. Low leptin and high ghrelin levels are linked to persistent problems with weight loss.

By stabilizing these hormone levels, low-carb dieting may circumvent hormonal resistance to weight loss experienced over multiple diet attempts. Further, research finds that low-carb diets help maintain lean muscle mass better than other diets during weight loss, preserving metabolic function.

Additional support for how carbohydrates are specifically processed explains why reducing them aids fat loss. After a carb-containing meal, increases in insulin inactivate the hormone-sensitive lipase responsible for releasing fatty acids from fat cells and activating lipogenesis instead. Long-term consumption of a high-carb, low-fat diet raises total cholesterol and triglyceride levels and lowers protective HDL cholesterol due to chronically elevated insulin overriding lipolysis. However, adhering to a low-carb way of eating lowers insulin levels, allowing triglycerides and fatty acid release from fat stores through increased hormone-sensitive lipase activity to provide energy to the tissues rather than relying on carbs.

Studies also show that ketone production from burning fat provides a better sense of fullness compared to glucose from carbs, likely from alterations in appetite-regulating hormones like ghrelin, CCK, GLP-1 and PYY. In addition, low-carb diets have been shown to upregulate fat-burning gene expression and downregulate fat-storing gene expression in the body. On a physiological level, the reduction of insulin antagonism of lipolysis combined with induction of lipolysis and ketone production is what gives low-carb meal plans their metabolic advantage for encouraging fat breakdown versus storage.

Key Benefits of a Low Carb Diet for Weight Management

From the scientific evidence, it is clear that low carbohydrate diets aid weight loss by modulating insulin sensitivity, hormone levels and gene expression in a way that shifts the body's metabolism towards fat-burning. Some of the key advantages that make adopting a low-carb lifestyle beneficial for successful and lasting weight management include the following:

- Fewer insulin spikes resulting from limited carb intake means the body has less opportunity to turn excess glucose into new fat cells via fat storage/de novo lipogenesis pathways. With less frequent high insulin levels, dieters feel fuller for longer and crave carbs less due to reduced effects on appetite-regulating hormones.

- Ongoing fat burning is supported by raised blood ketone levels produced when the liver breaks down stored and dietary fat into ketone bodies to use as fuel instead of relying on glucose. Maintaining nutritional ketosis prevents the body from using fat as its main energy source. Crop rotation is practiced to replenish soil
- nutrients and deter pests naturally
- Enhanced appetite control derived from stable blood sugar and leptin/ghrelin fluctuations makes low carbers feel satisfied on fewer daily calories. Lower hunger and improved satiety help dieters follow the low-carb plan long-term.
- Preservation of lean muscle mass during weight reduction due to less muscle protein breakdown compared to high carb, calorie deficient diets enables dieter metabolism to remain efficient for continual fat loss.
- Healthy cholesterol profile shifts through decreased total and LDL cholesterol and heightened protective HDL levels over time on a low-carb pattern.
- Potential reduction of risk factors for cardiometabolic disease markers like blood pressure, triglycerides and inflammation when adhering to nutrient-dense, whole-carb foods.

Decreased Fat Storage Through Lower Insulin Spikes

One of the primary reasons low-carb diets are so effective for losing weight is because they minimize fat storage over time. When carbohydrate intake is high, it triggers sharp rises in both blood sugar and insulin levels after meals. These frequent insulin spikes have a direct impact on fat accumulation in the body.

Insulin is a fat-storage hormone - it signals fat cells to take up blood glucose and convert it into triglycerides, which are then stored away as body fat. Consuming a diet low in carbs means blood sugar and insulin levels do not fluctuate as drastically after eating. There are fewer instances where excess glucose needs to be processed, so less fat is deposited.

The less frequent and extreme insulin responses from a lower-carb meal plan prevent excess glucose from being shunted into fat cells on an ongoing basis via de novo lipogenesis pathways. Over months and years, this reduced fat deposition leads to noticeable weight loss benefits. Clinical trials have shown low-carb dieters lose, on average, over twice as much weight in 6 months compared to low-fat dieters despite similar calorie intake. By minimizing new fat production and storage signals, a low-carb approach facilitates effective fat loss.

Improved Appetite Control and Fewer Cravings

In addition to less fat storage, low-carb diets aid weight management through enhanced appetite regulation. Constant blood sugar spikes and subsequent drops that come from a high-carb diet cause hunger and appetite-controlling hormones like ghrelin and leptin to fluctuate wildly. This triggers increased feelings of hunger between meals and carb cravings.

But, limiting dietary carbs stabilizes blood glucose levels, so these hormone fluctuations are minimized. Ghrelin remains low, while leptin stays elevated on a low-carb plan. Appetite is rebalanced, reducing excessive overeating urges. Studies show low-carb diets tend to decrease hunger and control appetite to a greater degree than other eating patterns.

Combined with choosing more satisfying proteins and fats, restricted carb intake ensures fullness lasts longer on fewer calories consumed naturally each day. This sustainable satiety is a hallmark of low-carb weight loss adherence and long-term success. Stable energy levels and minimized snacking behaviors aid in significant calorie reduction without feeling deprived.

Preserved Metabolic Rate and Lean Muscle Mass

Another notable benefit of low-carb dieting relates to lean muscle retention compared to other weight loss methods. Lower body protein loss means a faster metabolism is sustained during weight reduction efforts. More muscle equates to increased daily calorie burn potential, even at rest.

Clinical research has demonstrated that carb plans induce less lean tissue degradation than strictly calorie-controlled diets, especially higher carb formulations. This is partly because low-carb intake supports stable blood sugar and adequate intake of high-quality protein to maintain muscle.

By obtaining gluconeogenic precursors and key nutrients for muscle preservation from non-carb food sources, low-carb diets circumvent typical protein catabolism seen with aggressive calorie deficits. This muscle-sparing aspect upholds a high metabolism conducive to continuing fat loss success in the long term.

Optimized Gene Expression and Hormone Levels

The low-carb diet's physiological impacts extend beyond appetite and metabolism mechanisms. Studies show carb restriction alters fat storage and fat-burning gene expression profiles favorably. Genes involved in de novo lipogenesis and adipocyte hyperplasia are downregulated, while those tied to beta-oxidation and lipolysis are upregulated.

Additionally, adherence to a low-carb meal plan leads to heightened levels of fat-mobilizing hormones like adiponectin, decreased insulin-promoting hormones, and advantageous changes in other regulators like leptin and ghrelin, as discussed. These shifts help explain improved fat loss outcomes for low-carb adherents.

On a molecular level, the body dynamically responds to carb limitation by optimizing its internal environment and signaling at a genetic level to preferentially release and oxidize fatty acids instead of activating fat growth and storage pathways. These regulated changes aid prolonged fat loss success and maintenance of results over the lifespan.

Facilitation of Nutritional Ketosis

By consistently restricting dietary net carbs to levels inducing ketosis (around 50 grams daily or less), the low-carb diet delivers another distinct benefit. When fewer than 30-50g net carbs per day are consumed, the liver produces ketone bodies from fat to use as fuel instead of glucose.

This state of nutritional ketosis, achieved through fatty acid mobilization and ketogenesis rather than starvation, supports appetite control and preserves lean muscle mass even better than gluconeogenesis alone. It also enhances mental focus and energy levels for improved diet compliance in the long term despite fat adaptation.

Most significantly, ketosis primes the body for optimal fat burning by upregulating fat oxidizing enzymes and downregulating glucose dependency genes in metabolic tissues long term. Sustained ketosis underpins the low-carb diet's success at facilitating ongoing fat loss and maintaining results.

Chapter 2
Embracing Organic for Better Health

What Does "Organic" Truly Mean?

The term "organic" has become increasingly common when describing certain foods, but what does it actually mean? At its core, organic refers to a holistic approach to farming and food production that aims to work in harmony with nature rather than against it.

Specifically, organic agriculture focuses on environmental stewardship, promoting biodiversity and avoiding the use of synthetic chemical inputs like pesticides, antibiotics and genetically modified organisms (GMOs). Instead of relying on quick chemical fixes, organic farmers utilize prevention-focused practices that foster soil health and provide safe, high-quality food.

Some key principles of organic farming include using natural fertilizers derived from compost, manure or green manure crops rather than synthetic petroleum-based ones. Crop rotation is a natural way to restore soil nutrients and keep pests away. Livestock is able to graze on open pasture and cannot be given antibiotics, growth hormones or fed animal by-products (which conventional livestock often is).

Overall, the organic methodology aims to cultivate complete farm ecosystems that are sustainable and promote the well-being of both humans and the environment. Chemical-intensive conventional methods are eschewed in favor of working in cooperative harmony with natural cycles and balances. Integrated pest management with techniques like using beneficial insects is favored over routine pesticide spraying.

In addition to following strict production standards, farmers pursuing organic certification undergo regular on-site inspections by independent organizations to ensure compliance. Products bearing the USDA Organic seal must contain at least 95% certified organic ingredients. While certification is not mandatory for small or direct-to-consumer farms, the practices are still fundamentally organic in nature.

The organic concept stresses long-term soil health rather than short-term production yields that can deplete nutrients. Purposefully avoiding synthetic chemicals benefits the environment as they can accumulate and spread through waterways and ecosystems. It also prevents consumer exposure to potentially harmful residues in foods.

Ultimately, "organic" epitomizes a conscientious food philosophy where sustainable farming, environmental protection and human nutrition are inextricably linked. It moves beyond just not using synthetic inputs but fostering biodiverse landscapes where crops and livestock can live naturally balanced lives. And consumers can feel good knowing organic verified foods were grown without potentially harmful additives.

So, while organic may cost more for farmers due to less crop treatment dependency, the practices protect invaluable long-term resources and provide safe, highly nutritious foods. That is what the term truly encapsulates - a holistic, ethical approach benefiting people and the planet for generations to come through nourishing harmony with nature rather than antagonistic intervention against it.

Nutritional Benefits of Organic Foods

A growing body of research shows that organic produce and meat tend to have a more favorable nutrient profile than conventional varieties. Several key vitamins, minerals and antioxidants are often found at higher levels in organic foods. One review of dozens of studies found organic crops, on average, contained significantly higher concentrations of antioxidants like polyphenols. Antioxidants are important for disease prevention and support overall well-being. Higher antioxidant intake through organic fruits and vegetables may help offset cellular damage from environmental toxins we encounter daily. /Organic produce is also commonly higher in vitamins C and E, magnesium, phosphorus and other antioxidants like anthocyanins. For example, a study of apples found organic varieties provided approximately 50% more antioxidants overall versus conventional. Organic fruits and vegetables have higher quantities of antioxidants and vitamins, making them more nutrient-dense.

Nutrient Density of Organic Produce

One of the most well-documented nutritional benefits of organic foods is their higher density of vitamins, minerals and antioxidants compared to conventionally grown crops. Several factors contribute to this superior nutrient profile of organic produce.

First, organic soils treated with natural fertilizers like compost are richer in beneficial microbes and minerals that plants readily take up through their roots. Without the depletion caused by synthetic petroleum-based fertilizers, organic soils maintain higher levels of nutrients.

Second, the biodiversity encouraged by organic practices allows for optimal nutrient cycling. Cover crops, mulching and crop rotation all work to retain and replenish soil quality. This holistic approach means organic crops access abundant nutrients continuously from living, biologically active soil.

Numerous peer-reviewed studies have demonstrated higher nutrient levels across a variety of organic fruits and vegetables:

- Organic tomatoes, on average, contained 21-51% higher levels of the antioxidant lycopene compared to conventional tomatoes. Lycopene is essential for preventing illness.
- Organic peaches were found to have 25% more vitamin C, while organic pears had 13% more vitamin C than their conventionally grown counterparts. Vitamin C bolsters immunity and overall health.
- Higher concentrations of vitamin K, a key factor in bone health, were identified in organic lettuce varieties versus non-organic lettuce in one University of Washington study.
- Other nutrients organic produce surpasses conventional in include magnesium, copper, phosphorus and antioxidants like polyphenols and flavonoids. All are important cofactors for metabolic function and protection against cellular stressors.

The consistency of these research findings points to organic cultivation yielding foods inherently higher in protective vitamins, minerals, and plant compounds our bodies require for optimal physiological performance. Maximizing micronutrient intake is fundamental to health maintenance and disease avoidance.

Antioxidants and Health Benefits of Organic

A major focus of studies into organic food nutritional composition involves antioxidant levels. Antioxidants are incredibly important for human wellness as they defend cells from potentially damaging free radicals generated during metabolic processes.

One review published in the British Journal of Nutrition analyzed 343 peer-reviewed studies comparing antioxidant concentrations in organic and conventional crops. It determined organic fruits and vegetables had, on average, 18-69% higher antioxidant activity than conventionally grown foods. The most abundant antioxidants in many plant foods are polyphenols. Studies have found organic blueberries have 26% more polyphenols, and strawberries contain 28% higher levels of these cell-protecting compounds versus non-organic varieties.

Why is this organic antioxidant advantage crucial? Researchers theorize that consuming higher amounts of free radical-fighting antioxidants from organic sources may counteract oxidative stress caused by modern environmental pollutants and lifestyles. Simply put, organic antioxidants give our bodies a valuable boost, protecting us from DNA, nerve and cell membrane damage over the long term.

Nutritional Benefits of Organic Meat and Dairy

While produce receives the most scrutiny, research likewise shows notable wellness variances between organic and conventional animal products:

- Organically raised chickens without antibiotic overuse were found to have over 50% higher levels of heart-healthy omega-3 fatty acids versus conventional counterparts.
- Milk from organic grass-fed cows contains up to 60% more beneficial CLA fatty acids yet less saturated fat than milk from grain-fed cows. CLA has anti-inflammatory effects.

- Researchers found organically produced eggs contained about 10% less cholesterol, higher vitamin E and beneficial fatty acids compared to standard supermarket eggs.

These differences arise because organic standards prohibit non-therapeutic antibiotic use, growth hormones and confined animal feeding operations where animals primarily eat grains instead of grazing naturally. Pasture-raised organic livestock diets are closer to their evolutionary diets, providing more balanced nutrient profiles passed to consumers.

Overall Impact on Health

When considering the cumulative benefits of higher vitamin, mineral, antioxidant and healthy fat intake from a predominantly organic whole foods diet, the positive implications for health protection and disease risk reduction are enormous.

Organic nutrition fosters optimal physiological function at the cellular level, boosts immunity through natural compounds, and reduces oxidative stress throughout the entire body. Well-planned organic vegan or omnivorous diets are linked to lower incidences of obesity, diabetes, cancer and cardiovascular disease over the long term.

By emphasizing pesticide-free produce, sustainable animal products without artificial additions, and supporting small family farms, organic nutrition is about so much more than just food. It encapsulates a conscientious lifestyle protecting personal, community and environmental wellness for generations to come.

How Organic Complements Weight Loss Goals

While there is not yet definitive research showing organic diets directly cause weight loss, many factors of organic nutrition complement efforts to lose weight and maintain a healthy figure. At the root, choosing organic means avoiding unnecessary synthetic toxins while maximizing nutrient intake – both keys to optimal metabolism and weight regulation over the long term.

Avoiding Toxins Supports Weight Control

Synthetic pesticides used in conventional farming are increasingly linked to health issues like hormone disruption and metabolic dysfunction. Higher amounts of pesticide residue in non-organic diets have been linked in studies to increased waist circumference and body mass index (BMI) over time. Researchers believe this could be due to pesticides interfering with hormones and cells that regulate weight.

Going organic removes this source of toxicity. The body can better manage weight naturally without copious synthetic stresses. Organic supporters also point out that pesticides may alter gut bacteria, which plays a role in weight through appetite and fat storage impact. Choosing organic fosters a gut environment better able to aid balanced weight.

Nutrient Density Keep Satiety Higher for Longer

Higher antioxidant and vitamin levels in organic improve overall wellness, as the body's natural functions for regulating appetite and metabolism work optimally. Organic foods' superior nutrient profiles also mean they are more satiating.

Fibre, protein, healthy fats and other nutrients in organic fruits, vegetables and meat fill you up efficiently. This curbs overeating and helps maintain steady blood sugar levels, which is important for controlling hunger cues between meals. Studies confirm organic diets tend to rate higher on satiety scales, keeping appetites in check effortlessly, which aids weight maintenance in the long run.

Avoiding Hormones Optimizes Body's Own Signals

For meat and dairy, going organic removes artificial hormones from the picture. Conventional livestock are often given hormones to rapidly increase growth and milk production. However, studies find hormone residue consumption may disrupt our endocrine system's natural signals related to hunger, fat storage and more.

Organic meat and dairy let the body use only its own hormone signals to healthily manage appetite and metabolism. Following the body's natural cues facilitates weight control versus synthetic hormone disruption, which can subversively influence weight gains over time.

Less Processing Means Fewer Empty Calories

While not all organic food is inherently less processed, choosing organic often means selecting more whole, minimally packaged options. Highly processed convenience foods are linked to weight issues, as they are engineered to be hyper-palatable yet nutritionally vacant.

The fiber, protein and nutrients in organic whole foods suppress appetite much more effectively than added sugars, unhealthy oils and refined carbohydrates in processed snacks. Eating organic helps lock in nutrients for energy versus empty calories that get stored as fat. Less processed organic options satisfy both health and weight goals simultaneously.

Sustainable Practices Complement Healthy Lifestyle

Organic farming promotes environmental sustainability through natural methods that work with nature instead of against it. Like the renewable energy and low-waste movements, organic represents a mindful, balanced lifestyle tuned with the health of both people and the planet.

Following organic principles sets the foundation for optimal wellness at all levels - from the cellular to the community level. Choosing organic food aligns well with other positive health behaviors like regular exercise and stress management. Taking a holistic approach to lifestyle factors positions the body for long-term success, keeping weight balanced naturally.

By addressing weight issues from multiple angles with organic removal of toxins and nutrient density, appetite control support and less processing, regulating figures becomes an agreeable side effect versus a constant struggle. Because organic eating provides the body with everything it needs naturally to manage metabolism and hunger optimally, this is widely seen as one of organic nutrition's key contributions to sustaining a healthy weight over the lifespan.

Embracing Organic for Better Health

Overall, the research indicates organic nutrition delivers superior wellness benefits that enable our inherent ability to maintain a healthy figure. Choosing organic means avoiding synthetic chemicals from conventional practices that can disrupt hormones and metabolism related to weight regulation over time.

Maximizing nutrient intake through the density of organic fruits, vegetables, and humanely-raised meat/dairy optimizes overall cellular health so the body can naturally burn calories efficiently and feel full between meals to curb overeating. Organic also pairs well with a balanced lifestyle involving regular exercise and managing stress, further supporting satiety and metabolic well-being.

By taking a preventative, holistic approach through organic eating, weight control ceases to feel like a constant battle, as our inherent weight wisdom can instead work effectively unimpeded. Of course, individual metabolism and genetics still play a role in size and shape, but the research suggests organic provides vibrant fuel and removes interferences so the body's natural weight equilibrium mechanisms function at their best.

In the end, embracing organic farming's natural philosophy allows us to nourish our bodies, giving them what they truly need without unnecessary synthetic alterations. This sets the optimal conditions for wellness at all levels, including helping maintain a healthy weight, leaving us feeling energized and at ease within our natural size and appearance designed to thrive. The numerous documented benefits position organic as an ideal complementary choice for both general and weight-specific health goals in the long term.

Chapter 3
Setting Yourself Up for Success

Personalizing Your Carb Intake

Adopting a low-carb lifestyle means finding the right carb intake level for your individual body and goals. It's important to start by tracking your carb consumption to determine your daily limit. Begin by cutting back on obvious sources like bread, pasta and sugar. Pay close attention to how you feel both physically and mentally over the first few weeks at different intake levels. Things like energy levels, hunger, cravings and weight loss progress can help identify your optimal range.

Finding the Right Level

When first starting a low-carb diet, it's ideal to gradually reduce your carb intake to find your optimal level. Keeping a food log is crucial in this process, as it allows you to carefully monitor how different amounts of carbs make you feel both physically and mentally. As a starting point, aim to cut out obvious high-carb foods like pasta, bread, potatoes and sugary snacks. Track your intake for 1-2 weeks at a moderately reduced level, such as 100-150g net carbs per day. Keep a close eye on any changes in your mood, appetite, desires, and energy levels.

As you log your food and gather feedback from your body, look for patterns that emerge at a certain carb intake threshold. Do you tend to feel more lethargic or irritable above 120g, for example? Above this amount, do you notice increased cravings kicking in? Is your digestion better than 100g? Learning where your threshold lies can take trial and error. But, paying attention to subtle cues will provide invaluable insights. You may also start to see differences in your weight loss progress at lower versus higher intakes within your initial testing range.

After your first few weeks of monitoring, you can gradually reduce your daily carb limit by 5-10g. Continue tracking diligently to see how your body reacts at the lower level for 1-2 more weeks. Repeat this process of gradual reduction paired with close self-observation until you feel your energy, satiety and mood are optimized. Most people settle in with the best results, eating 20-150g net carbs per day. However, your personal range may be narrower based on your feedback. Be patient through the adjustment stage, allowing a few weeks at each level to give your metabolism time to recalibrate. Listening to what your specific needs and preferences are will empower you to determine a limit tailored for long-lasting, sustainable weight management. Choosing an intake environment where your body thrives sets the stage for success.

Adjusting Over Time

As your journey progresses and weight loss goals change, it's common for your carb needs to evolve as well. While a very low initial intake of under 20g carbs daily jumpstarts fat adaption, long-term such an extreme reduction can feel socially limiting or lead to cravings. Most dietitians advise narrowing in on a personal limit in the range of 20-150g net carbs as a healthy target, which may vary slightly over time. Once you reach the later stages of your weight loss with just 10-15 pounds remaining, you can start increasing your carb intake slowly at 5-10g increments. Watch for signs your metabolism can tolerate slight increases without stalling progress. Pay attention to how another 5g of sweet potato or fruit makes you feel. If weight still comes off steadily and your energy levels stay regulated, keep raising it gradually until stabilization occurs. The amount that will maintain results shifts smaller as goals are almost complete.

As maintenance becomes the priority after goal weight achievement, further increases in moderation may support long-term adherence. Monitor changes for 2-4 weeks at new levels to confirm continued balance. With the right adjustments guided by self-awareness over months and years, your low-carb lifestyle can remain flexible and naturally adaptive based on your evolving needs.

Personalizing Through Monitoring

When first embarking on self-monitoring, start by tracking carbs, protein, fat, calories and fiber intake daily using an app or food log. Weighing all foods provides the most accurate data. Record any additional factors that seem tied to your performance, like measurements, estrogen cycle, stool consistency, mood and activity levels. Note these details alongside carb amounts eaten to look for relations.

As you compile personal data points over 8-12 weeks, review entries for trends that stand out. Excel or similar programs allow organizing inputs into visual charts for patterns to emerge more easily. Correlate high intake occasions to related variables and vice versa. Through diligent tracking and analytical reflection, you inform the reduction strategy most individualized for your circumstances - whether it's hitting a refined carb limit specifically or trimming 50 calories on workout days, as examples. Armed with deep self-awareness from committed monitoring, proactively course correct when starting to feel "off." Precise adjustments keep you feeling energized and satisfied for a long time. Periodic reassessments every 3-6 months reconfirm continued alignment as your setup naturally optimizes further over the long run.

Recognizing and Overcoming Weight Loss Plateaus

Our bodies undergo adaptive changes when starting a new lifestyle, like low-carb eating. Seeing a lack of progress can be discouraging if not properly understood. Recognizing stalls are temporary due to biological factors, not personal failings, is key to overcoming them successfully long-term.

One challenge many low-carb followers face is weight loss plateaus. It's important to recognize that plateaus are a normal part of any weight loss journey that can last 2-6 weeks. During a stall period, your body is adjusting to your new lifestyle. Before making any dietary or habit adjustments, exercise patience and stick to your regular schedule. Adding extra calories through increases in portion sizes or lower-quality carbs will likely prolong the plateau.

Assessing Contributing Factors

Some factors that can contribute to a plateau period include hydration levels, sleep, stress levels and menstrual cycles in women. Evaluate accompanying lifestyle stresses that may be contributing to the stall. Are stress levels elevated or activity decreased? Addressing stressors through relaxation and maintaining sufficient activity aids in an ideal recovery environment and could help push through adaptation changes quickly. Make sure to drink plenty of water, aim for 7-9 hours of sleep per night, implement relaxation techniques and be aware of hormonal timing. These aspects of your lifestyle have a big impact on your metabolism. After maintaining your low-carb routine conscientiously for 4-6 weeks with no progress, there are some strategies you can try to break through a stall. Slightly reducing calorie intake by cutting back on oils or increasing activity may restart loss. You can also try incorporating short-term intermittent fasting to shock your system. Other techniques involve changing up your macro ratio by reducing protein or fat slightly for added carb flexibility.

If nothing has worked after 6-8 weeks, it may be time to consider having your hormones and thyroid levels tested by a doctor. Occasionally, underlying medical conditions need to be addressed. But patience is still important - stay consistent while exploring potential issues since your weight loss should eventually resume once your body fully adapts. With persistence and appropriate adjustments over time, you will successfully move past each plateau toward your goal.

Tools and Trackers to Monitor Progress

Self-monitoring offers powerful individualized insights driving strategic progress when implemented consistently yet flexibly long-term. Through diligent yet customized tracking combined with community involvement, underlying patterns emerge, unveiling the most optimized approach. This supports continuous personalization of your lifestyle catered to evolving needs promoted by deeper self-awareness over time. Monitoring ultimately nourishes long-lasting transformation driven by nurturing your whole well-being.

Monitoring Your Progress

Carefully tracking your progress is vital for long-term success in any lifestyle change program. Not only does it allow you to monitor weight fluctuations over time, but it also provides insight into other positive transformations occurring in your body and habits that a scale cannot detect. This holistic view keeps you motivated by celebrating all types of victories, large and small. With diligent self-monitoring customized to your needs, you empower yourself to continuously optimize your individualized approach.

Why Self-Monitoring Is Important

When embarking on a new way of eating, like low carb, gaining deep self-awareness through consistent tracking is key. It informs you of how your body specifically responds both physically and mentally to various factors like macronutrient intake, meals, exercise, sleep and stress. Patterns that emerge from collected data points over weeks and months guide strategic adjustments personalized to your circumstances. This tailored feedback loop supports sustainable progress catered to your unique biochemistry and priorities.

Setting Up an Effective System

To set up an organized yet easy self-monitoring system, determine what types of inputs and outputs are most relevant to your goals. Tracking weight fluctuations is standard, but also noting measurements, fitness stats, energy/mood ratings, return of problematic health symptoms and progress photos capture different successes. Investing in an intuitive app specialized to your needs streamlines logging food, water and active living entries seamlessly each day. Popular options for low-carb tracking include MyFitnessPal, Cronometer and CarbManager, as well as tailored to macro counting. Wearable tech additions like Fitbit or Garmin help log steps, heart rate, sleep metrics and workouts effortlessly, too, when synced. A simple journal supplements electronic data collection to jot subjective, non-quantitative notes about your experiences and insights each week. The organization, through dedicated sections by category, keeps all aspects logically grouped.

Reviewing Metrics for Patterns

Preparing bi-weekly, monthly or longer summary reports allows for spotting trends across variables over time. Take recorded inputs and filter views of the raw data through Excel pivot table organization and conditional highlighting. This customized analysis presents relationships between factors more clearly for uncovering actionable takeaways.

For example, a busy period showed higher stress ratings coupled with increased carb intake and diminished activity compared to baseline. Or a spike in energy occurred following a bout of intermittent fasting. Unearthing such correlations indicating when certain behaviors, periods or stressors may undermine your system empowers proactive course correcting before a plateau sets in. This precision helps optimize progress continually.

Leveraging Technology Support Systems

Pairing data compilation with online community involvement maintains accountability throughout the journey. Whether in private Facebook groups or public subreddits, sharing both triumphs and setbacks with like-minded individuals boosts morale and motivation. Crowdsourcing advice on navigating challenging times from those, further along prevents feelings of isolation that could derail determination. Health coaching services also augment independent initiatives through video consultations. Professionals are uniquely qualified to interpret biometric readings and guide tailored adjustments informed by objective analyses. This guided support increases understanding with a partnership approach versus feelings of being left to fend entirely alone subjective interpretations.

Making Monitoring Sustainable

While diligent tracking demands regular commitment, find enjoyable integrated habits promoting adherence long-term. Meal prep on Sundays with nutritional info logged in one sitting saves time. Brief daily entries during morning coffee or evening wind-down flow naturally. Monthly "report card" days celebrate yourself through reflection versus feeling like a chore. Customizable goal celebration rewards maintain excitement, like a walking concert or a new fitness outfit. Tracking empowers rather than restricts through a focus on sustainable lifestyle and wellness over numbers alone. Consistency with a positive mindset nurtures continued success on your journey.

Chapter 4
The Importance of Whole Foods

Beyond "Low Carb": The Pitfalls of Processed Foods

While drastically reducing carbohydrate intake can lead to rapid, short-term weight loss, focusing solely on lowering carb grams often means replacing healthy whole foods with highly processed substitutes. Although these packaged products may boast of having few carbs or being low in calories, they typically lack nutrients and negatively impact health. Maintaining a healthy weight over time requires making dietary decisions that feed our bodies from the inside out.

Weight management requires more than just counting macros. Consuming highly processed fare, even if low in carbs and calories, disrupts our natural hunger and fullness cues. Without fiber, protein and fat from whole foods, our bodies cannot feel satisfied after eating. We may eat far more than intended, trying to feel full, sabotaging weight goals. Artificial flavors and sweeteners confuse our taste buds and sugar cravings, leading to overconsumption. Additionally lacking in vitamins, minerals, and antioxidants that our bodies require to operate at their best and correctly metabolise food are these synthetic replacements.

The Lack of Nutrients in Ultra-Processed Items

Highly processed "low-carb" foods are low in density despite purported low calorie/carb counts. They have been stripped of essential vitamins, minerals, fiber, antioxidants and beneficial plant compounds through fractionation and reformulation. Without these important building blocks, our bodies cannot function optimally. Real foods work synergistically to support long-term health.

The Metabolic Impact of Fiber Deficiency

Fiber plays a key role in regulating appetite and blood sugar levels. Deficient diets focused on processed low-carb foods lack this nutrient and dysregulate hormones like insulin. This disruption of hormonal signals leads to frequent overeating to feel satisfied. Fibre is also crucial for a balanced gut microbiome that influences metabolism.

Sweet Cravings and Hormonal Imbalances

Artificial sweeteners and flavors in packaged substitutes undermine our natural preferences for nutrients while promoting tendencies for sugary tastes. They disrupt leptin and ghrelin, hormones controlling appetite. Healthy fats are also needed to produce serotonin, yet they are often replaced with inflammatory oils in ultra-processed fare.

Prioritizing Whole, Minimally Processed Foods

For sustained weight management and overall well-being, real foods that nourish us from within must take priority. These include quality proteins, complex carbs, and beneficial fats from natural, plant-based sources. This supports stable blood sugar, prolongs satiety, and enables effortless wellness for the long term.

Focusing on Nutrient Density

To effectively achieve and maintain a healthy weight long-term, focusing solely on calorie and macronutrient counts is ineffective. A much better strategy is concentrating on the nutrient density of foods. Nutrient density refers to the variety of essential vitamins, minerals, antioxidants and fiber provided per calorie. Choosing whole, minimally processed foods with high nutrient loads naturally supports satiation and wellness in a sustainable way.

For the calories consumed, whole meals like fresh fruits and vegetables offer the most nutritional value. Produce is naturally low in energy density due to water and fiber content yet high in an extensive array of antioxidants and other important compounds. Just a small amount leaves us feeling satisfied yet provides key nutrients that fuel our cells and regulate processes like metabolism. Antioxidants quench free radicals, combating oxidative stress and damage over time.

Fibre is crucial to weight management as it aids digestion and feeds beneficial gut bacteria linked to good health. Getting adequate fiber is challenging at a calorie deficit, but produce ensures intake is met. Fibre optimizes nutrient absorption while prolonging the emptying of the stomach, inducing a sense of fullness with very few calories. High-carb, processed snacks may be low-calorie but lack fiber, nutrients and satiety.

Lean proteins high in nutrients include fish, poultry, eggs, lentils, and nuts. Optimal protein intake is important for preserving metabolism and muscle mass during weight loss to prevent rebound weight gain. Complete proteins provide all essential amino acids needed in balanced amounts. Pairing proteins with fibrous carbs and fats at meals controls appetite naturally for hours via balanced blood sugar and insulin levels.

Healthy fats from sources such as olive oil, avocados, coconut and nuts are increasingly recognized for their positive impact on satiety and weight regulation. Fat is compulsory for the absorption of fat-soluble vitamins and also the production of hormones that balance hunger signals. Monounsaturated fatty acids have anti-inflammatory benefits as well. Getting fats from whole foods versus trans or saturated options is important.

The Role of Natural Fats in Satiety and Weight Loss

For many years, fats were demonized as the enemy of weight loss efforts due to their high-calorie content. However, recent research has revealed that including the right types of natural fats can actually enhance feelings of fullness and aid in weight management. Contrary to popular belief, avoiding all fats is counterproductive, and certain fatty foods can promote satiety when consumed in moderation. This chapter will explore the mechanisms by which fats induce satiety and support sustainable weight control when obtained from whole, minimally processed food sources.

How Fats Support Satiety

One of the key ways fats aid satiety is by slowing digestion. While carbohydrates and proteins are emptied from the stomach relatively quickly, fats take longer to break down and digest. This prolongs the time between eating and hunger recurring, allowing the eater to feel full for extended periods. Studies show that meals or snacks containing a balance of protein, carbs, and healthy fats result in steadier blood sugar levels as well. Balanced blood sugar prevents spikes and crashes that can trigger overeating. The sustained energy helps curb appetite and cravings between meals.; Fats also directly signal the brain that they are filling us up. Key players in this process are the satiety hormones PYY and CCK, which are released from the gut during digestion in response to fatty acid intake. Research indicates that oleic acid, the predominant fatty acid in oils like olive and avocado, has the strongest effect on increasing levels of these hormones compared to other macronutrients. Meals including a moderate amount of fat are more effective at inducing fullness than low-fat fare due to the enhancement of this satiety response. Without adequate fat, we may overeat more quickly, trying to feel satisfied, which can easily undermine weight goals.

Whole Food Sources of Beneficial Fats

Certain high-fat, whole foods are especially effective for promoting feelings of volume and satiation. Avocados are a prime example, as they contain almost double the fat of eggs by weight but fewer overall calories thanks to the fiber and water content. Their creamy texture stems from healthy monounsaturated fat, shown to aid fullness hormones the most. Other nutritious plant-based sources of monounsaturated fat include coconut, nuts and seeds. These foods provide an array of appetite-suppressing fats, fiber, protein and micronutrients working synergistically to maximize the feeling of fullness per calorie. Fatty fish also richly supply omega-3 fats important for neurological and hormonal health.

Nutrient Absorption and Optimal Wellness

Dietary fat serves several essential metabolic roles beyond satiety. It facilitates the absorption of fat-soluble vitamins A, D, E and K from foods, as well as antioxidants, allowing the body to derive maximum benefit. Additionally, the brain and hormone function are directly supported by omega-3 fatty acids like EPA and DHA. Conducting a thorough examination of all currently available food items and ingredients is the first step. Adequate intake is needed to produce serotonin, a neurotransmitter regulating mood, appetite and sleep cycles. Mental wellness fosters behaviors that are conducive to sustainable weight regulation. Further, whole food fats provide energy and optimize cellular function when consumed as part of an overall nutritious diet.

Sustained Weight Management

Numerous factors contribute to long-term weight management success. Feeling satisfied between meals prevents consuming excess calories that can thwart goals. Balanced blood sugar and steady energy curve hunger and cravings. Metabolic balancing optimizes calorie burning, avoiding plateaus. A positive mindset prevails over deprivation or rebound tendencies. Studies show these outcomes are supported at a nutritional level by including high-quality dietary fats. As an integral component of a real food diet, fats help keep pounds off for good when appropriately managed.

Appropriate Portion Sizing is Key

While naturally present fats aid fat loss, appropriate portions are still necessary for weight control success. Isolated fatty acids or excess portions can undermine the calorie balance required for weight management if overconsumed. The key is obtaining fats primarily from whole sources, which provide fiber, protein, vitamins and minerals to feel full in moderate amounts. Also, focusing on monounsaturated varieties abundant in plant foods supports health while mitigating some calorie impact. With careful, strategic sizing, science demonstrates beneficial fats fully compatible with a nutritious weight loss regimen.

Chapter 5
Adapting to an Organic Low Carb Lifestyle

Organizing Your Organic Low Carb Kitchen

A well-laid-out kitchen is an essential component for achieving long-term success on an organic, low-carb diet. It allows for meals to be prepared with minimal hassle while ensuring healthy options are always at hand. Taking the time to thoughtfully arrange cabinets, counters and refrigerator space based on your dietary needs pays dividends in staying on track long term.

The first step is to do a complete audit of all current food items and ingredients. Thoroughly inspect packages and labels, removing anything with significant amounts of refined carbohydrates, added sugars or unhealthy fats. Outdated or expired items should be discarded as well to avoid clutter. This purge will free up valuable real estate for healthier, low-carb staples. Resist the urge to replace with imitation substitutes. Instead, focus cabinet space on whole, nutrient-dense basics.

Dry goods like nuts, seeds, nut butter and dried coconut should have a dedicated space near the main work area for convenient snacking. These energy-boosting ingredients are versatile additions to both sweet and savory dishes. Ensure oils are near the cooktop for easy access. Coconut, olive and avocado oils are heart-healthy fats for both raw and cooked preparations. The baking aisle can house items like almond and coconut flour for grain-free recipes. Canned foods provide portable protein options for last-minute meals. Tuna, salmon, sardines and bone broth are ideal for this section.

Fruit and vegetable crispers demand special attention to maximize longevity. Produce tends to last longest when stored appropriately. Washing, spinning dry, and packing leafy greens like spinach and kale into bags or containers is recommended. To prevent cross-contamination, store meat on the lower shelves and bake on the upper shelves. Berries are best kept in the original clamshell versus pouring loose in bins where they can crush each other. Potatoes, onions and winter squashes have the longest shelf life when placed in a dry, dark spot. Organize by type and use by dates to avoid waste.

The expansive refrigerator real estate is best utilized with these priorities in mind. Door shelves hold condiments while the main body focuses on core ingredients. Veggie and salad prep are organized by type in drawers- carrots in one, broccoli in another, for example. This approach keeps similar items bundled for easy access. The meat compartment displays protein options like eggs, poultry, fish and grass-fed beef. Hard cheeses, plain Greek yogurt, and butter or ghee round out daily dishes.

Within the fridge and freezer, implemented organization leads to order and off-the-cuff healthy choices. Meal prep of chopped veggies, boiled eggs or roasted meat saves time and money with little effort. Labeled containers of homemade bone broth, soups or chilis guarantee a warm meal is never far away. Over time, maintaining a purposeful and clean kitchen makes sticking to an organic, low-carb lifestyle second nature rather than a constant burden. With the right arrangement, wholesome eating flourishes with minimal stress.

Pantry Organization:

- Group similar ingredients together on shelves for logical flow. For example, nuts, seeds, and dried fruit together.
- Keep most used staples like coconut flour and almond flour at eye level for convenience.
- Label glass jars or bins for bulk items like oats and nut butter to keep track of contents and dates.
- Use pull-out shelves, baskets or bins to corral items and utilize vertical space fully.

Fridge Organization:

- Designate crisper drawers - one for veggies, one for fruits.
- Place yogurt eggs in the main body above drawers for easy reach.
- Store meat on bottom shelves and bake on higher shelves to avoid cross-contamination.
- Portion protein and cheese into individual containers or bags for single-serve items.
- Label and date items to use first-in-first-out and reduce waste.

Freezer Organization:

- Reserve freezer space for whole cuts of grass-fed beef, wild fish or bone broths.
- Freeze homemade casserole slices, chili, and soup in individual containers for ease.
- Pop meal-prepped items into the freezer before leaving for the day to streamline.
- Create an inventory checklist of items to track what's stocked and needs replenishing.

Countertop Organization:

- Place frequently used items like cutting boards, knives, and pots within easy access.
- Store cookbook staples you refill, like olive oil, near the stovetop work area.
- Clear counters completely after cooking to avoid clutter interfering with cleanliness.

Budgeting Tips: Weight Loss on a Wallet-Friendly Diet

When adopting a long-term healthy eating lifestyle like an organic low-carb diet, budgeting is an important factor to consider. Maintaining the diet should not put a strain on finances or require expensive specialty foods. However, with some savvy shopping techniques and meal preparation strategies, you can easily lose weight while saving money at the grocery store.

One of the easiest methods to maximise nutrition for less money is to purchase produce that is in season. Fruits and vegetables that are abundant when locally harvested will be significantly cheaper than out-of-season imports. Check local farmer's markets, grocery store flyers and plant databases online to see what produce is regionally plentiful each month. For example, in the summer, you may fill your basket with affordable leafy greens, berries, peppers and tomatoes perfect for salads. In the winter, focus on root vegetables, winter squashes and cabbage, which are stored well for long-cooking recipes.

Buying meat and seafood in family-size packs or bulk can offer dramatic discounts, especially when items are on sale. To prevent waste later, portion and freeze what won't be used within three to four days. Cuts like chicken thighs or drumsticks, ground beef or bison, and wild-caught frozen fish or shrimp are budget-appropriate protein sources. When roasting or braising a large piece of meat on the weekend, be sure to cook extra to use in multiple meals throughout the week, like lettuce-wrapped tacos, salads or stir-fries. This stretches the protein further while avoiding repeat trips to the grocery.

Eggs should always have a regular place in your shopping cart as one of the most affordable, high-quality foods available. At about $3-4 per dozen (or just $0.25 each), eggs provide complete protein and keep you feeling full for hours. For breakfast, hard boil a batch on Sunday, then pack as snacks all week. Or whip up an omelet, frittata or quiche to enjoy throughout the week instead of costly morning pastries or cereals. Dried legumes, lentils and frozen cruciferous vegetables like cauliflower and broccoli are extremely inexpensive sources of fiber, nutrients and plant-based proteins. A 1lb bag of beans, which provides several servings, is typically $1-2. Frozen cauliflower "rice," riced broccoli, and zoodles are wonderful substitutes for higher-carb versions at a fraction of the cost. Always keep these on hand to create hearty, budget-friendly side dishes and main courses.

Making larger pots of bone broth from meaty animal bones is a thrifty way to gain joint-healthy collagen benefits. Ask your butcher for bones, which can often be obtained for free. Slow-simmering them all day infuses nourishing minerals into the broth at virtually no extra cost compared to store-bought. Sip broth plain or use in soups, stews and risottos for maximum economy.

Meal planning is key - Taking time on Sundays or at the beginning of each week to plan out recipes and snack ideas ensures all ingredients are purchased intentionally with minimal waste. Known quantities needed to prevent overbuying. Creating a weekly grocery list streamlines shopping efficiency.

Multi-purpose ingredients - Versatile foods like cabbage, cauliflower and salmon are invested in for multiple applications. Cabbage becomes salad, soup bases or kimchi. Cauliflower masquerades as mashed potatoes or pizza crust. Salmon provides breakfast, bento box items or light dinners.

Bulk cooking - Large roast chicken, meatloaf, frittatas or baked fish dishes are prepared to enjoy throughout the week. Individual portions can be frozen, ensuring that the productivity of time spent in the kitchen is maximized.

Seasonal sales - Stay aware of what may be marked down towards the end of its shelf life through reduced pricing. Broccoli, berries and stonefruit can often be had at half the original cost just before expiry.

Bento box prep - Portion-controlled snacks and lunches assembled in advance cut down on expensive mid-day options. Hard-boiled eggs, jerky, nut butter packets and cut veggies pack easily.

Pantry management - Check expiration dates and use first in/first out to reduce loss from neglecting older items. Clear shelf space periodically to keep up with current needs.

With diligent use of sales, seasonality and maximizing multi-use ingredients through bulk cooking, meal prep and planning, an organic diet remains very budget-conscious.

Dining Out and Socializing on Your Diet

Engaging in social activities and enjoying time with friends and family is an important part of overall well-being. But going to social events or eating out might provide new difficulties when on an organic low-carb diet. With some strategy and preparation, it is absolutely possible to stick to your nutrition plan while still participating fully in events.

When going to restaurants, the first step is to evaluate the menu ahead of time, either online or via a restaurant's website. Scan for protein-focused options that allow for substitutions. Look for dishes featuring simply prepared beef, poultry, fish or seafood, along with steamed or grilled non-starchy vegetables. As an alternative to carb-heavy sides, request double portions of the approved veggie sides instead. Many restaurants are accommodating of special requests to leave out rice, pasta or baked potatoes if notified in advance.

If appetizers are part of the plan, substitution ideas can keep you on track. Instead of bread or batter-fried choices, opt for a mixed green salad, seafood cocktail or vegetable crudites with a low-carb dip. You can also politely ask your server if any appetizers can be made with simple seasoning and grilling or roasting in place of breading or sugary sauces. Advocating for your needs upfront allows the kitchen staff to better assist.

When dining out, it's helpful to have a backup plan in case optimal options are limited. Consider bringing along certain portable low-carb snacks just in case, like beef jerky, hard-boiled eggs, roasted nuts or cheese. This ensures you aren't forced into an unsatisfying scenario due to a lack of choice or reliance on willpower alone. Pack discreetly so as not to detract from the dining experience of others. Staying well-hydrated with water is also important to avoid confusing hunger and thirst cues.

Attending social gatherings like barbecues, cocktail parties, or family celebrations need not compromise your health goals with a little forethought. Offer to bring a homemade low-carb dish as your contribution if hosting. Options like vegetable crudites, guacamole, jerky or extra grilled proteins pair perfectly with any spread. For potlucks, choose a green salad or roasted veggie platter that aligns with your diet, but plenty can be enjoyed. Pack a small cooler of approved snacks to nibble on so hunger doesn't tempt you to wander by high-starch dishes or dessert tables.

Parties often equate indulgence with food, but true enjoyment comes from social time. Shift focus from what's on the plates to engaging conversations instead. Explain your Culinary path simply if offered tempting morsels, then steer interaction topics elsewhere. Spending energy on connecting over shared interests and stories crowds out fixation on any forbidden foods present. Reminding loved ones you came to visit them, not sample the hors d'oeuvres, helps reframe goals for the event.

Responsible commitments like dining out or gatherings build invaluable social support networks. With discreet planning and graceful communication of needs, they satisfy obligations while staying true to nutrition priorities, too. Small adjustments make a world of difference in living fully within healthy restrictions in the long term. Overall, life balance does not require perfection - simply continual learning and effort where possible. Social accountability through positive examples can even inspire others on similar wellness journeys, too.

Chapter 6
Organic Low Carb Cookbook (100 recipes)

Disclaimer: *To truly benefit from the approach of this cookbook, every ingredient used in the recipes of this chapter must be organic. It is vital to ensure that the produce you purchase is genuinely organic. If you're new to a low-carb diet, consider discussing dietary changes with a nutritionist or healthcare provider.*

Shopping list

Here's a comprehensive shopping list that includes all the ingredients used in the recipes:

Vegetables and Fruits:

- Spinach leaves
- Kale leaves
- Cucumber
- Limes
- Strawberries
- Blueberries
- Raspberries
- Banana
- Avocados
- Ginger

- Mint leaves
- Mixed berries (strawberries, blueberries, raspberries)
- Coconut
- Lemons

Nuts and Seeds:

- Almonds
- Walnuts
- Macadamia nuts
- Chia seeds

Dairy and Dairy Alternatives:

- Greek yogurt
- Almond milk (unsweetened)

Coconut milk (unsweetened); Proteins:

- Eggs
- Meats (beef, lamb, pork, chicken)
- Wild-caught fish and seafood
- Chicken sausage
- Sausage (for tacos)
- Pork ribs

Healthy Fats:

- Olive oil
- Coconut oil
- Butter and ghee

Sweeteners:

- Honey

Herbs and Spices:

- Fresh basil leaves
- Vanilla extract

Others:

- Shredded coconut
- Coconut water (unsweetened)
- Mint leaves (for garnish)

Conversion table

Here's a conversion table for common European and American units of measurement:

Length:

- 1 meter (m) = 3.28084 feet (ft)
- 1 centimeter (cm) = 0.393701 inches (in)

Weight:

- 1 kilogram (kg) = 2.20462 pounds (lb)
- 1 gram (g) = 0.0352739 ounces (oz)

Volume:

- 1 liter (L) = 1.05669 quarts (qt)
- 1 liter (L) = 0.264172 gallons (gal)
- 1 milliliter (mL) = 0.033814 ounces (fl oz)

Temperature:

- Celsius (°C) to Fahrenheit (°F): $°F = (°C \times 9/5) + 32$

Liquid Volume:

- 1 milliliter (mL) = 0.001 liters (L)
- 1 liter (L) = 0.001 cubic meters (m³)
- 1 milliliter (mL) = 0.061024 cubic inches (in³)
- 1 liter (L) = 0.0353147 cubic feet (ft³)

Area:

- 1 square meter (m²) = 10.7639 square feet (ft²)
- 1 square centimeter (cm²) = 0.155000 square inches (in²)
- 1 hectare (ha) = 2.47105 acres

Liquid Capacity:

- 1 milliliter (mL) = 0.001 deciliters (dL)
- 1 liter (L) = 0.1 decaliters (daL)
- 1 liter (L) = 0.01 hectoliters (hL)

Mass (Weight):

- 1 gram (g) = 0.001 kilograms (kg)
- 1 kilogram (kg) = 35.274 ounces (oz)
- 1 kilogram (kg) = 2.20462 pounds (lb)

Cooking Measurements:

- 1 teaspoon (tsp) = 5 milliliters (mL)
- 1 tablespoon (tbsp) = 15 milliliters (mL)
- 1 fluid ounce (fl oz) = 29.5735 milliliters (mL)
- 1 cup (c) = 240 milliliters (mL)
- 1 pint (pt) = 473.176 milliliters (mL)
- 1 quart (qt) = 0.946353 liters (L)
- 1 gallon (gal) = 3.78541 liters (L)

BREAKFAST

Spinach and Feta Omelets

Time: 15 minutes
Preparation: 5 minutes
Servings: 2

INGREDIENTS

- 4 large eggs
- 2 cups fresh spinach, washed and chopped
- 1/2 cup feta cheese, crumbled
- 2 tablespoons olive oil
- Salt and black pepper to taste
- 1 tablespoon butter (for cooking)
- Chopped fresh herbs (such as parsley or chives, optional, for garnish)

INSTRUCTIONS

1. Prepare the Ingredients:
   - Crack the eggs into a bowl and whisk them until well beaten.
   - Season the beaten eggs with a pinch of salt and a dash of black pepper.
   - Tear up the feta cheese and chop the fresh spinach. Put them away. Set them aside.
2. Saute the Spinach:
   - In a non-stick skillet, heat 2 tablespoons of olive oil over medium heat.
   - Add the chopped spinach and sauté for about 2-3 minutes until it wilts and becomes tender. Season with a pinch of salt.
3. Create the Omelet Mixture:
   - Pour the beaten eggs over the sautéed spinach and allow them to cook for a minute or two without stirring. Use a spatula to lift the edges as they start to set and tilt the pan

so that the raw egg flows to the edges. Mix well and let it sit for 5-10 minutes to allow the chia seeds to thicken the yogurt

4. Add Feta Cheese:
   * Sprinkle the crumbled feta cheese evenly over one-half of the omelet.
5. Fold the Omelet:
   * Once the eggs are almost fully set but still slightly runny on top, gently fold the other half of the omelet over the cheese side using a spatula.
6. Cook to Perfection:
   * Lower the heat and cook for an additional 1-2 minutes until the omelet is cooked through and the cheese melts.
7. Serve:
   * Carefully slide the spinach and feta omelet onto a plate.
   * Garnish with fresh chopped herbs if desired.

Nutritional Values (per serving): Calories: 260 Kcal; Protein: 14g; Carbohydrates: 4g; Fat: 20g

Coconut Yogurt with Mixed Berries

Time: 10 minutes
Preparation: 10 minutes
Servings: 2

INGREDIENTS

* 1 cup coconut yogurt (unsweetened)
* 1/2 cup mixed berries (such as strawberries, blueberries, and raspberries)
* 2 tablespoons chia seeds
* 1 tablespoon coconut flakes (for garnish, optional)
* 1 teaspoon honey or a sugar-free sweetener (optional for added sweetness)

INSTRUCTIONS

1. Prepare the Ingredients:
   * Wash and pat dry the mixed berries. Set them aside.
   * In a bowl, combine the coconut yogurt and chia seeds. Stir thoroughly, then set aside for five to ten minutes so the chia seeds can thicken the yoghurt.

2. Layer the Yogurt and Berries:
   * Start by spooning a layer of the chia-infused coconut yogurt into two serving glasses or bowls.
3. Add the Mixed Berries:
   * Top the yogurt layer with a portion of the mixed berries.
4. Repeat the Layers:
   * Add another layer of yogurt and another portion of mixed berries.
5. Garnish:
   * If desired, sprinkle a few coconut flakes on top for extra flavor and texture.
6. Sweeten (Optional):
   * If you prefer your dessert a bit sweeter, drizzle a teaspoon of honey or a sugar-free sweetener over the top.
7. Serve:
   * Serve your Coconut Yogurt with Mixed Berries immediately, or refrigerate for a short while to chill.

Nutritional Values (per serving): Calories: 160 Kcal; Protein: 5g; Carbohydrates: 15g; Fat: 10g

Kale and Avocado Scrambled Eggs

Time: 15 minutes
Preparation: 5 minutes
Servings: 2

INGREDIENTS

* 4 large eggs
* 2 cups fresh kale, washed and chopped
* 1 ripe avocado, diced
* 2 tablespoons olive oil
* Salt and black pepper to taste
* 1/4 cup shredded cheese (optional, for garnish)
* Chopped fresh herbs (such as parsley or cilantro, optional, for garnish)

INSTRUCTIONS

1. Prepare the Ingredients:
   * Crack the eggs into a bowl and whisk them until well beaten. Season with a pinch of salt and a dash of black pepper.
   * After giving the kale a good wash, trim off

any tough stems, and slice it into small pieces.
  - Dice the ripe avocado and set it aside.
2. Saute the Kale:
  - Heat 2 tablespoons of olive oil in a skillet over medium heat.
  - After adding the chopped kale, sauté it for two to three minutes, or until it wilts and gets soft. Add a little salt and pepper for seasoning.
3. Add Avocado:
  - Once the kale is tender, add the diced avocado to the skillet. Gently stir to combine with the kale.
4. Scramble the Eggs:
  - Pour the beaten eggs over the sautéed kale and avocado. Allow them to simmer for a minute or two without stirring.
5. Garnish with Cheese (Optional):
  - If desired, sprinkle a bit of shredded cheese on top of the eggs.
6. Continuously Scramble:
  - Use a spatula to gently scramble the eggs, mixing them with the kale and avocado until the eggs are cooked to your preferred level of doneness.
7. Serve:
  - Carefully transfer the Kale and Avocado Scrambled Eggs to plates.
  - Garnish with fresh chopped herbs if desired.

Nutritional Values (per serving): Calories: 320 Kcal; Protein: 15g; Carbohydrates: 6g; Fat: 25g

Zucchini Pancakes with Butter

Time: 20 minutes
Preparation: 10 minutes
Servings: 2

INGREDIENTS

- For the Zucchini Pancakes:
- 2 medium-sized zucchinis, grated
- 2 large eggs
- 1/4 cup almond flour
- 1/4 cup grated Parmesan cheese
- 2 cloves garlic, minced
- 1/4 teaspoon dried basil
- Salt and black pepper to taste
- 2 tablespoons olive oil (for cooking)
- For Serving:
- 2 tablespoons butter
- Fresh basil leaves (for garnish, optional)

INSTRUCTIONS

1. Prepare the Zucchini:
  - Grate the zucchini using a box grater, then place the grated zucchini in a clean kitchen towel or cheesecloth and squeeze out excess moisture.
2. Create the Pancake Batter:
  - In a mixing bowl, combine the grated zucchini, eggs, almond flour, grated Parmesan cheese, minced garlic, dried basil, salt, and black pepper. Mix everything together until well combined.
3. Cook the Pancakes:
  - Heat 2 tablespoons of olive oil in a non-stick skillet over medium heat.
  - Spoon some of the zucchini pancake batter into the skillet using a ladle or measuring cup. Utilising the spoon's back, distribute it into a circular form. Continue until there are as many pancakes in the skillet without it becoming crowded.
4. Fry Until Golden Brown:
  - Cook the pancakes for about 2-3 minutes on each side until they are golden brown and crispy.
5. Serve with Butter:
  - Transfer the zucchini pancakes to serving plates. Top each with a generous dollop of butter.
6. Garnish (Optional):
  - If desired, garnish with fresh basil leaves for a pop of color and flavor.

Nutritional Values (per serving): Calories: 280 Kcal; Protein: 11g; Carbohydrates: 10g; Fat: 21g

Asparagus and Cheese Frittata

Time: 30 minutes
Preparation: 10 minutes
Servings: 2

INGREDIENTS

- 6 large eggs
- 1/2 pound fresh asparagus, tough ends removed, and cut into 1-inch pieces
- 1/2 cup shredded cheese (choose your favorite variety, such as cheddar, mozzarella, or Gruyere)
- 2 tablespoons olive oil
- 2 tablespoons butter
- 1/4 cup milk or milk alternative (unsweetened)
- Salt and black pepper to taste
- Fresh herbs (such as chives or parsley, for garnish, optional)

INSTRUCTIONS

1. Prepare the Ingredients:
   - Crack the eggs into a bowl and whisk them until well beaten. Add the milk, salt, and black pepper, and whisk again. Set aside.
   - Preheat your oven's broiler.
2. Saute the Asparagus:
   - In an oven-safe skillet, heat 2 tablespoons of olive oil over medium heat.
   - After adding the asparagus pieces, sauté them for three to four minutes, or until they are soft and starting to caramelise.
   - Add a little salt and pepper for seasoning.
3. Add Eggs and Cheese:
   - Reduce the heat to low and pour the beaten egg mixture over the sautéed asparagus.
   - Sprinkle the shredded cheese evenly over the eggs.
4. Cook on the Stovetop:
   - Allow the frittata to cook without stirring for 4-5 minutes or until the edges are set but the center is still slightly runny.
5. Finish Under the Broiler:
   - Place the skillet under the broiler for 2-3 minutes until the frittata puffs up and the top is golden and set.
6. Garnish and Serve:
   - Carefully remove the frittata from the oven. Garnish with fresh herbs if desired.
   - Cut and serve straight from the skillet, or move to a platter.

Nutritional Values (per serving): Calories: 350 Kcal; Protein: 17g; Carbohydrates: 7g; Fat: 26g

Broccoli and Chicken Sausage Breakfast Casserole

Time: 45 minutes
Preparation: 15 minutes
Servings: 4-6

INGREDIENTS

- For the Casserole:
- 6 eggs
- 1/2 cup almond milk (unsweetened)
- 12 ounces chicken sausage links, sliced
- 2 cups fresh broccoli florets, blanched and drained
- 1 cup shredded cheese (choose your favorite variety)
- 1/2 teaspoon garlic powder
- Salt and black pepper to taste
- 1 tablespoon olive oil (for greasing the dish)
- For Topping (optional):
- Sliced green onions
- Chopped fresh herbs (such as parsley or chives)
- Salsa (sugar-free, if preferred)

INSTRUCTIONS

1. Preheat the Oven:
   - Preheat your oven to 375°F (190°C).
2. Prepare the Ingredients:
   - In a large bowl, whisk together the eggs and almond milk until well combined. Add black pepper, garlic powder, and salt for seasoning.
   - Heat one tablespoon of olive oil in a pan over medium heat. When the chicken sausage is well cooked and browned, add the slices and sauté. Take off the heat and place aside. Remove from heat and set aside.
   - Blanch the broccoli florets in boiling water for 2-3 minutes, then drain and set aside.

3. Assemble the Casserole:
   - Grease a baking dish with olive oil to prevent sticking.
   - Spread the blanched broccoli florets evenly in the bottom of the dish.
   - Scatter the cooked chicken sausage over the broccoli.
   - Pour the egg and almond milk mixture over the sausage and broccoli.
   - Sprinkle the shredded cheese on top.
4. Bake:
   - Place the baking dish in the preheated oven and bake for approximately 25-30 minutes, or until the casserole is set and the top is golden brown.
5. Garnish and Serve:
   - Once done, remove the casserole from the oven. Garnish with sliced green onions, chopped herbs, or salsa if desired.
   - Slice and serve directly from the dish.

Nutritional Values (per serving, assuming 4 servings): Calories: 350 Kcal; Protein: 22g; Carbohydrates: 6g; Fat: 25g

Flaxseed Breakfast Porridge with Almond Milk

Time: 15 minutes
Preparation: 5 minutes
Servings: 2

INGREDIENTS

- 1/2 cup ground flaxseeds
- 2 cups unsweetened almond milk
- 1/4 cup chopped nuts (such as almonds or walnuts)
- 1/4 cup fresh berries (such as blueberries or raspberries)
- 1 tablespoon chia seeds
- 1/2 teaspoon vanilla extract
- 1/2 teaspoon cinnamon
- 1 tablespoon honey or a sugar-free sweetener (optional for added sweetness)
- Fresh berries (for garnish, optional)

INSTRUCTIONS

1. Prepare the Ingredients:
   - In a bowl, combine the ground flaxseeds, almond milk, chia seeds, vanilla extract, and cinnamon. Mix well and let it sit for 5 minutes to allow the mixture to thicken.
2. Warm the Porridge:
   - Transfer the flaxseed mixture to a saucepan and warm it over low heat. Stir continuously to prevent sticking or burning.
3. Simmer and Thicken:
   - As the mixture heats, it will begin to thicken. Continue to simmer and stir for about 5 minutes until the porridge reaches your desired thickness.
4. Add Toppings:
   - Once the porridge is ready, remove it from the heat. Stir in the chopped nuts and fresh berries. If you prefer a sweeter taste, add a tablespoon of honey or a sugar-free sweetener.
5. Garnish (Optional):
   - If desired, garnish your Flaxseed Breakfast Porridge with additional fresh berries and a sprinkle of nuts.
6. Serve:
   - Spoon the warm porridge into bowls and serve immediately.

Nutritional Values (per serving): Calories: 300 Kcal; Protein: 10g; Carbohydrates: 14g; Fat: 20g

Coconut Flour Waffles

Cooking Time: 10 minutes
Preparation Time: 10 minutes
Portions: 2 people

INGREDIENTS

- 1/2 cup coconut flour
- 4 large eggs
- 1/4 cup coconut milk
- 2 tablespoons coconut oil, melted
- 1/2 teaspoon baking powder
- 1/4 teaspoon sea salt
- 1/2 teaspoon pure vanilla extract
- Coconut oil or cooking spray for waffle iron

INSTRUCTIONS

1. Preheat Your Waffle Iron:
   - Start by preheating your waffle iron according to the manufacturer's instructions. This will ensure your waffles cook evenly and don't stick.
2. Mix Dry Ingredients:
   - In a mixing bowl, combine the coconut flour, baking powder, and sea salt. Mix them well, ensuring there are no lumps in the coconut flour.
3. Whisk Wet Ingredients:
   - In another bowl, whisk the eggs until they are well beaten. Add the coconut milk, melted coconut oil, and pure vanilla extract. Mix until you have a smooth, well-combined wet mixture.
4. Combine Wet and Dry Mixtures:
   - Pour the wet mixture into the bowl with the dry ingredients. Stir until you have a thick, smooth batter. The coconut flour will absorb the moisture and thicken the batter.
5. Grease the Waffle Iron:
   - Lightly grease the waffle iron with coconut oil or cooking spray. This step prevents the waffles from sticking and adds a subtle coconut flavor.
6. Cook the Waffles:
   - Pour the batter onto the preheated waffle iron, spreading it evenly. Close the lid and cook until the waffles are golden brown and slightly crisp. Cooking time may vary depending on your waffle iron.
7. Serve Warm:
   - Carefully remove the waffles from the iron and place them on a plate. Serve the coconut flour waffles warm.

Nutritional Values (per serving): Calories: 298 Kcal; Protein: 12g; Carbohydrates: 11g; Fat: 23g

Coconut and Blueberry Muffins

Time: 30 minutes
Preparation: 10 minutes
Baking: 20 minutes
Servings: 12 muffins

INGREDIENTS

- 1 1/2 cups coconut flour
- 1/2 cup almond flour
- 1/2 cup unsweetened shredded coconut
- 2 teaspoons baking powder
- 1/2 teaspoon salt
- 1/2 cup coconut oil, melted
- 1/4 cup honey or a sugar-free sweetener (adjust to taste)
- 4 eggs
- 1 cup unsweetened almond milk
- 1 teaspoon vanilla extract
- 1 cup fresh blueberries

INSTRUCTIONS

1. Preheat the Oven:
   - Set the oven temperature to 175°C, or 350°F.
   - Line a muffin tin with paper liners or grease the muffin cups with a bit of coconut oil.
2. Mix the Dry Ingredients:
   - In a large mixing bowl, combine the coconut flour, almond flour, shredded coconut, baking powder, and salt. Mix well to combine all the dry ingredients.
3. Combine the Wet Ingredients:
   - In another bowl, whisk together the melted coconut oil, honey or sugar-free sweetener, eggs, almond milk, and vanilla extract until the mixture is well combined.
4. Combine Wet and Dry Mixtures:
   - Pour the wet ingredients into the bowl with the dry ingredients. Stir until you have a smooth batter.
5. Fold in Blueberries:
   - Gently fold the fresh blueberries into the muffin batter.
6. Fill Muffin Cups:
   - Using a spoon or scoop, fill each muffin cup about 2/3 full with the muffin batter.

7. Bake:
   - Place the muffin tin in the preheated oven and bake for approximately 20 minutes, or until the muffins are golden brown and a toothpick inserted into the center of a muffin comes out clean.
8. Cool and Serve:
   - Allow the muffins to cool in the muffin tin for a few minutes, then transfer them to a wire rack to cool completely.

Nutritional Values (per muffin, assuming 12 muffins): Calories: 200 Kcal; Protein: 4g; Carbohydrates: 12g; Fat: 15g

Smoked Salmon and Cream Cheese Roll-Ups

Time: 15 minutes
Preparation: 15 minutes
Servings: 4

INGREDIENTS

- 4 ounces smoked salmon
- 4 ounces of cream cheese
- 2 green onions, thinly sliced
- 1 tablespoon fresh dill, chopped
- 1 teaspoon lemon juice
- Salt and black pepper to taste
- Cucumber slices (optional, for serving)

INSTRUCTIONS

1. Prepare the Ingredients:
   - In a bowl, soften the cream cheese at room temperature for a few minutes to make it easier to work with.
   - Thinly slice the green onions, chop the dill, and squeeze the lemon juice.
2. Mix the Cream Cheese Filling:
   - In a mixing bowl, combine the softened cream cheese, sliced green onions, chopped dill, lemon juice, a pinch of salt, and a dash of black pepper. Mix until well combined.
3. Assemble the Roll-Ups:
   - Lay out a sheet of plastic wrap on your work surface.
   - Lay the smoked salmon slices flat on the plastic wrap, slightly overlapping each other, to form a larger rectangular sheet.
   - Spread the cream cheese mixture evenly over the smoked salmon.
4. Roll the Roll-Ups:
   - Starting from one edge, carefully and tightly roll up the smoked salmon with the cream cheese mixture inside. Use the plastic wrap to help keep the roll compact.
5. Chill and Slice:
   - Place the roll in the refrigerator for at least 15-20 minutes to firm up.
   - Once chilled, remove the plastic wrap and slice the roll into bite-sized pieces.
6. Serve:
   - Serve the Smoked Salmon and Cream Cheese Roll-Ups on a platter, garnished with additional dill and optionally with thin slices of cucumber.

Nutritional Values (per serving, assuming 4 servings): Calories: 160 Kcal; Protein: 8g; Carbohydrates: 2g; Fat: 13g

Avocado and Bacon Breakfast Skillet

Time: 20 minutes
Preparation: 10 minutes
Cooking: 10 minutes
Servings: 2

INGREDIENTS

- 4 slices of bacon, chopped
- 2 ripe avocados, pitted and diced
- 4 eggs
- 1/2 cup cherry tomatoes, halved
- 1/4 cup red onion, finely chopped
- 1/4 cup bell peppers (red, yellow, or green), diced
- 1 tablespoon olive oil
- Salt and black pepper to taste
- Fresh cilantro or parsley (for garnish, optional)

INSTRUCTIONS

1. Cook the Bacon:
   - In a large skillet, cook the chopped bacon over medium heat until it becomes crispy.

Once done, remove it from the skillet and set it aside.

2. Sauté the Veggies:
   - In the same skillet, add 1 tablespoon of olive oil and heat it over medium heat.
   - Add the finely chopped red onion and diced bell peppers. They should become fragrant after a few minutes of sautéing.

3. Add Eggs and Avocado:
   - Create small wells in the skillet by pushing aside the sautéed vegetables.
   - Crack the eggs into the wells, one in each well.
   - Carefully distribute the diced avocado around the eggs.
   - Season the eggs with salt and black pepper.

4. Cook Until Eggs Set:
   - Cover the skillet and let the eggs cook for about 5-6 minutes until the egg whites are set and the yolks are cooked to your desired level of doneness.

5. Add Tomatoes and Bacon:
   - Once the eggs are nearly done, scatter the halved cherry tomatoes and the previously cooked bacon over the skillet.

6. Garnish and Serve:
   - Garnish your Avocado and Bacon Breakfast Skillet with fresh cilantro or parsley if desired.
   - Serve the skillet directly from the pan while it's still hot.

Nutritional Values (per serving, assuming 2 servings): Calories: 400 Kcal; Protein: 15g; Carbohydrates: 15g; Fat: 32g

Sautéed Kale and Poached Eggs

Time: 20 minutes
Preparation: 10 minutes
Cooking: 10 minutes
Servings: 2

INGREDIENTS

- For Sautéed Kale:
- 4 cups kale leaves, washed and chopped
- 2 cloves garlic, minced
- 2 tablespoons olive oil
- Salt and black pepper to taste
- 1/4 teaspoon red pepper flakes (optional, for a hint of spice)
- For Poached Eggs:
- 4 large eggs
- 1 tablespoon white vinegar (for poaching)
- Salt and black pepper to taste

INSTRUCTIONS

Sautéed Kale:
1. Sauté the Kale:
   - In a skillet, heat 2 tablespoons of olive oil over medium heat.
   - Add the minced garlic and sauté for about 30 seconds until fragrant.
   - Add the chopped kale leaves and sauté for 4-5 minutes, stirring occasionally, until they wilt and become tender.
   - Season with salt, black pepper, and red pepper flakes if desired.

Poached Eggs:
1. Bring Water to a Simmer:
   - In a wide saucepan, bring about 3 inches of water to a gentle simmer. Add 1 tablespoon of white vinegar to the simmering water.
2. Crack and Poach Eggs:
   - Crack each egg into a small bowl or cup. Gently create a whirlpool in the simmering water using a spoon.
   - Carefully slide each egg into the center of the whirlpool. The swirling water helps the egg whites wrap around the yolks.
   - Poach the eggs for about 3-4 minutes for a runny yolk or longer for a firmer yolk.
3. Remove and Season:
   - Use a slotted spoon to remove the poached eggs from the water, allowing any excess water to drain.
   - To taste, add a dash of salt and black pepper for seasoning.

Assemble:
1. Serve:
   - Divide the sautéed kale between two plates.
   - Place two poached eggs on top of the sautéed kale on each plate.
   - Garnish with additional black pepper and red pepper flakes if desired.

Nutritional Values (per serving, assuming 2

servings): Calories: 180 Kcal; Protein: 12g; Carbohydrates: 8g; Fat: 12g

Almond and Raspberry Breakfast Smoothie

Time: 5 minutes
Preparation: 5 minutes
Servings: 2

INGREDIENTS

- 1 cup fresh or frozen raspberries
- 1 cup unsweetened almond milk
- 1/2 cup Greek yogurt (unsweetened)
- 1/4 cup almond butter
- 1 tablespoon chia seeds
- 1/2 teaspoon vanilla extract
- 1-2 tablespoons honey or a sugar-free sweetener (adjust to taste)
- Ice cubes (optional, for extra chill)

INSTRUCTIONS

1. Combine Ingredients:
   - In a blender, combine the raspberries, almond milk, Greek yogurt, almond butter, chia seeds, and vanilla extract.
2. Sweeten and Blend:
   - Add the honey or sugar-free sweetener to the blender, adjusting to your preferred level of sweetness.
   - If you prefer a colder smoothie, add a few ice cubes.
   - Blend everything until the mixture is smooth and well combined.
3. Taste and Adjust:
   - Taste the smoothie and adjust the sweetness or consistency by adding more honey, almond milk, or ice cubes if needed.
4. Serve:
   - Pour the Almond and Raspberry Breakfast Smoothie into two glasses.
   - Optionally, garnish with a few extra raspberries or a sprinkle of chia seeds.

Nutritional Values (per serving, assuming 2 servings): Calories: 280 Kcal; Protein: 9g; Carbohydrates: 18g; Fat: 20g

Chia Seed and Strawberry Breakfast Pudding

Time: 10 minutes (plus chilling time)
Preparation: 10 minutes
Chilling: 2-4 hours (or overnight)
Servings: 2

INGREDIENTS

- 1 cup unsweetened almond milk
- 1/4 cup chia seeds
- 1/2 teaspoon vanilla extract
- 1-2 tablespoons honey or a sugar-free sweetener (adjust to taste)
- 1 cup strawberries, hulled and sliced
- Fresh mint leaves (for garnish, optional)

INSTRUCTIONS

1. Mix the Chia Seed Base:
   - In a mixing bowl, combine the almond milk, chia seeds, vanilla extract, and honey or sugar-free sweetener. Stir well to thoroughly combine the ingredients.
2. Add Strawberries:
   - Gently fold in the sliced strawberries. Reserve a few slices for garnish if desired.
3. Chill:
   - Cover the bowl with plastic wrap and refrigerate for at least 2-4 hours or overnight. This enables the liquid to seep into the chia seeds, giving them a pudding-like consistency.
4. Stir and Serve:
   - Before serving, give the pudding a good stir to evenly distribute the strawberries and ensure a creamy consistency.
5. Garnish:
   - Optionally, garnish your Chia Seed and Strawberry Breakfast Pudding with fresh mint leaves and reserved strawberry slices.

Nutritional Values (per serving, assuming 2 servings): Calories: 180 Kcal; Protein: 4g; Carbohydrates: 20g; Fat: 10g

Cauliflower Hash Browns

Time: 30 minutes
Preparation: 15 minutes
Cooking: 15 minutes
Servings: 4

INGREDIENTS

- 1 medium-sized cauliflower head, grated (about 4 cups)
- 1/2 cup grated cheese (your choice, such as cheddar or mozzarella)
- 2 eggs
- 1/4 cup almond flour
- 2 cloves garlic, minced
- 1/2 teaspoon garlic powder
- 1/2 teaspoon onion powder
- Salt and black pepper to taste
- 2-3 tablespoons olive oil (for cooking)

INSTRUCTIONS

1. Prepare the Cauliflower:
   - Wash and grate the cauliflower using a box grater. Alternatively, you can pulse the cauliflower in a food processor until it reaches a rice-like consistency.
   - Place the grated cauliflower in a clean kitchen towel or cheesecloth and squeeze out excess moisture.
2. Mix the Hash Brown Mixture:
   - In a large mixing bowl, combine the grated cauliflower, grated cheese, eggs, almond flour, minced garlic, garlic powder, onion powder, salt, and black pepper. Mix until all ingredients are well combined.
3. Form Hash Browns:
   - Divide the mixture into 4 equal portions. Take each portion and form it into a patty or hash brown shape with your hands.
4. Cook the Hash Browns:
   - Heat olive oil in a big skillet over medium heat.
   - Carefully place the cauliflower hash brown patties into the skillet.
   - Cook for about 3-4 minutes on each side or until they are golden brown and crispy.
5. Serve:
   - Once done, transfer the cauliflower hash browns to a plate lined with paper towels to remove excess oil.
   - Serve your Cauliflower Hash Browns hot as a side dish or a low-carb breakfast option.

Nutritional Values (per serving, assuming 4 servings): Calories: 180 Kcal; Protein: 8g; Carbohydrates: 8g; Fat: 12g

Sausage and Bell Pepper Breakfast Tacos (with Lettuce Wrap)

Time: 20 minutes
Preparation: 10 minutes
Cooking: 10 minutes
Servings: 4

INGREDIENTS

- 1 pound breakfast sausage (pork or chicken), casings removed
- 1 bell pepper, diced
- 1/2 red onion, diced
- 1 teaspoon olive oil
- 8 large lettuce leaves (such as iceberg or Romaine)
- 4 eggs
- Salt and black pepper to taste
- 1/2 cup shredded cheese (your choice, such as cheddar or pepper jack)
- Salsa (organic and sugar-free, if preferred)
- Fresh cilantro (for garnish, optional)

INSTRUCTIONS

1. Sauté the Sausage and Veggies:
   - Heat olive oil in a big skillet over medium heat.
   - Add the sausage, breaking it up with a spatula as it cooks. Cook until browned and cooked through.
   - Add the diced bell pepper and red onion. They should become fragrant after a few minutes of sautéing. Season with salt and black pepper.
2. Prepare the Lettuce Wraps:
   - Carefully separate the large lettuce leaves

and wash them. These will be your taco shells.

3. Scramble the Eggs:
   - In a separate pan, scramble the eggs in a bit of olive oil or butter until they're just set.
4. Assemble the Tacos:
   - To assemble each taco, start with a lettuce leaf as the "taco shell."
   - Spoon the sausage and vegetable mixture into the lettuce leaf.
   - Top with scrambled eggs, shredded cheese, and a dollop of salsa.
5. Garnish and Serve:
   - Garnish your Sausage and Bell Pepper Breakfast Tacos with fresh cilantro if desired.
   - Serve immediately.

Nutritional Values (per serving, assuming 4 servings): Calories: 350 Kcal; Protein: 18g; Carbohydrates: 5g; Fat: 28g

Mixed Nut Granola with Coconut Milk

Time: 30 minutes
Preparation: 10 minutes
Baking: 20 minutes
Servings: 8

INGREDIENTS

- 2 cups mixed nuts (e.g., almonds, walnuts, pecans), roughly chopped
- 1/2 cup unsweetened shredded coconut
- 1/4 cup chia seeds
- 1/4 cup flaxseeds
- 1/4 cup pumpkin seeds
- 1/4 cup sunflower seeds
- 1/4 cup coconut oil, melted
- 1/4 cup honey or a sugar-free sweetener (adjust to taste)
- 1 teaspoon vanilla extract
- 1/2 teaspoon cinnamon
- Pinch of salt
- Coconut milk (unsweetened, for serving)

INSTRUCTIONS

1. Preheat the Oven:
   - Preheat your oven to 325°F (163°C).
   - Line a baking sheet with parchment paper.
2. Prepare the Dry Ingredients:
   - In a large mixing bowl, combine the mixed nuts, shredded coconut, chia seeds, flaxseeds, pumpkin seeds, and sunflower seeds. Mix well.
3. Prepare the Wet Ingredients:
   - In a separate bowl, mix the melted coconut oil, honey or sugar-free sweetener, vanilla extract, cinnamon, and a pinch of salt.
4. Combine Wet and Dry Mixtures:
   - Pour the wet mixture over the dry ingredients and stir until everything is well-coated.
5. Bake the Granola:
   - Spread the granola mixture evenly on the prepared baking sheet.
   - Bake in the preheated oven for about 20 minutes, or until it turns golden brown, stirring every 5-10 minutes to ensure even baking.
6. Cool and Store:
   - Allow the granola to cool completely on the baking sheet. It will keep getting crisper as it cools.
   - After the granola cools, break it into clusters and store it in an airtight container.
7. Serve:
   - Serve your Mixed Nut Granola with Coconut Milk in a bowl, topped with unsweetened coconut milk.

Nutritional Values (per serving, assuming 8 servings without coconut milk): Calories: 280 Kcal; Protein: 6g; Carbohydrates: 12g; Fat: 23g

Grilled Chicken Caesar Salad with Kale and Homemade Dressing

Time: 30 minutes
Preparation: 15 minutes
Cooking: 15 minutes
Servings: 2

INGREDIENTS

- For the Grilled Chicken:
- 2 boneless, skinless chicken breasts
- 1 tablespoon olive oil
- Salt and black pepper to taste
- 1/2 teaspoon garlic powder
- 1/2 teaspoon onion powder
- 1/2 teaspoon paprika
- For the Salad:
- 4 cups kale, chopped
- 1/2 cup cherry tomatoes, halved
- 1/4 cup grated Parmesan cheese
- Croutons (optional, for serving)
- Lemon wedges (for serving)

- For the Homemade Caesar Dressing:
- 1/2 cup mayonnaise
- 1/4 cup grated Parmesan cheese
- 2 tablespoons lemon juice
- 2 cloves garlic, minced
- 1 teaspoon Dijon mustard
- 1/2 teaspoon Worcestershire sauce
- Salt and black pepper to taste

INSTRUCTIONS

Grilled Chicken:
1. Preheat Grill:
   - Set your grill's temperature to medium-high.
2. Season Chicken:
   - Rub the chicken breasts with olive oil, salt, black pepper, garlic powder, onion powder, and paprika.
3. Grill Chicken:
   - Grill the chicken for about 6-7 minutes per side, or until the internal temperature
   - Before slicing, take the chicken off the grill and let it a few minutes to rest.

Homemade Caesar Dressing:

1. Mix Dressing:
   - In a bowl, whisk together the mayonnaise, grated Parmesan cheese, lemon juice, minced garlic, Dijon mustard, Worcestershire sauce, salt, and black pepper. Adjust the seasonings to your taste.

Salad Assembly:

1. Prepare the Kale:
   - In a large bowl, place the chopped kale. Drizzle with a small amount of the Caesar dressing and massage the dressing into the kale leaves for a few minutes. This helps to soften the kale.
2. Assemble Salad:
   - Add the halved cherry tomatoes and grated Parmesan cheese to the kale.
   - Toss the salad with more of the Caesar dressing until well-coated.
3. Serve:
   - Divide the salad into two plates.
   - Top each salad with sliced grilled chicken.
   - Optionally, garnish with croutons and serve with lemon wedges on the side.

Nutritional Values (per serving, assuming 2 servings, without croutons): Calories: 450 Kcal; Protein: 40g; Carbohydrates: 10g; Fat: 25g

Broccoli and Cheddar Soup

Time: 30 minutes
Preparation: 10 minutes
Cooking: 20 minutes
Servings: 4

INGREDIENTS

- 4 cups broccoli florets (fresh or frozen)
- 1 small onion, diced
- 2 cloves garlic, minced
- 4 cups vegetable or chicken broth (low-sodium)
- 1 cup heavy cream or unsweetened almond milk for a lighter option
- 2 cups sharp cheddar cheese, grated
- 2 tablespoons butter or olive oil
- Salt and black pepper to taste
- A pinch of nutmeg (optional)
- Chives or green onions (for garnish, optional)

INSTRUCTIONS

1. Sauté Onions and Garlic:
   - In a large pot, melt the butter or heat the olive oil over medium heat.
   - Add the minced garlic and chopped onions. The onions should be sautéed for a few minutes to turn transparent.
2. Cook Broccoli:
   - Add the broccoli florets to the pot and sauté for another 5 minutes.
3. Add Broth and Simmer:
   - Pour in the vegetable or chicken broth.
   - After bringing the mixture to a boil, lower the temperature to a simmer. Cover and cook for about 15 minutes or until the broccoli is tender.
4. Blend the Soup:
   - Use an immersion blender or transfer the soup to a blender in batches to puree it until smooth.
   - If using a regular blender, be sure to allow the soup to cool slightly before blending.
5. Return to Pot:
   - Return the pureed soup to the pot.
6. Add Cream and Cheese:
   - Stir in the heavy cream or unsweetened almond milk.
   - Add the grated cheddar cheese to the soup gradually, stirring until it melts completely.
   - If desired, increase the flavour by adding a pinch of nutmeg.
7. Season and Serve:
   - Season the soup with salt and black pepper to taste.
   - Serve your Broccoli and Cheddar Soup hot, garnished with chopped chives or green onions if desired.

Nutritional Values (per serving, assuming 4 servings): Calories: 400 Kcal; Protein: 12g; Carbohydrates: 8g; Fat: 35g

Spinach and Avocado Salad with Olive Oil Dressing

Time: 15 minutes
Preparation: 15 minutes
Servings: 2

INGREDIENTS

- For the Salad:
- 6 cups baby spinach leaves
- 1 large avocado, peeled, pitted, and sliced
- 1/4 cup red onion, thinly sliced
- 1/4 cup cherry tomatoes, halved
- 2 tablespoons sunflower seeds (optional, for crunch)
- Feta cheese, crumbled (optional for garnish)
- For the Olive Oil Dressing:
- 3 tablespoons extra-virgin olive oil
- 2 tablespoons balsamic vinegar
- 1 clove garlic, minced
- 1 teaspoon Dijon mustard
- Salt and black pepper to taste

INSTRUCTIONS

Salad:

1. Prepare the Spinach:
   - Wash and dry the baby spinach leaves thoroughly, then place them in a large salad bowl.
2. Add Avocado and Veggies:
   - Add the sliced avocado, red onion, and cherry tomatoes to the spinach.
3. Add Optional Ingredients:
   - If desired, sprinkle sunflower seeds and crumbled feta cheese over the salad.

Olive Oil Dressing:

1. Prepare the Dressing:
   - Combine the extra-virgin olive oil, balsamic vinegar, Dijon mustard, minced garlic, salt, and black pepper in a small bowl. Mix well with a whisk.
2. Dress the Salad:
   - Drizzle the olive oil dressing over the salad.
3. Toss and Serve:
   - Gently toss the salad to evenly coat the ingredients with the dressing.

4. Garnish and Serve:
   - Optionally, garnish the salad with a bit more crumbled feta cheese or extra sunflower seeds.

Nutritional Values (per serving, assuming 2 servings, without optional ingredients): Calories: 300 Kcal; Protein: 4g; Carbohydrates: 10g; Fat: 27g

Zucchini Noodle and Prawn Aglio Olio

Time: 20 minutes
Preparation: 10 minutes
Cooking: 10 minutes
Servings: 2

INGREDIENTS

- 2 large zucchinis, spiralized into noodles
- 12-16 large prawns (shrimp), peeled and deveined
- 4 cloves garlic, minced
- 1/4 cup extra-virgin olive oil
- 1/2 teaspoon red pepper flakes (adjust to taste)
- Lemon zest (from 1 lemon)
- Lemon juice (from 1 lemon)
- Salt and black pepper to taste
- Fresh parsley, chopped (for garnish, optional)
- Grated Parmesan cheese (for garnish, optional)

INSTRUCTIONS

1. Prepare the Zucchini Noodles:
   - Spiralize the zucchini into noodles and set them aside.
2. Sauté the Prawns:
   - Heat 2 tablespoons of olive oil in a large skillet over medium-high heat.
   - After adding the prawns, sauté them for two to three minutes on each side, or until they are cooked through and turn pink.
   - After taking the prawns out of the skillet, set them aside.
3. Sauté the Garlic and Red Pepper Flakes:
   - In the same skillet, add the minced garlic and red pepper flakes.
   - After roughly a minute of sautéing, the garlic should smell fragrant but not browned.

4. Add Zucchini Noodles:
   - Add the spiralized zucchini noodles to the skillet.
   - Sauté for 2-3 minutes, tossing them with the garlic and red pepper flakes until they are slightly softened but still crisp-tender.
5. Combine the Dish:
   - Return the cooked prawns to the skillet with the zucchini noodles.
   - Add lemon zest and lemon juice.
   - Drizzle with the remaining olive oil.
   - Toss everything together to combine.
   - To taste, add salt and black pepper for seasoning.
6. Garnish and Serve:
   - Optionally, garnish your Zucchini Noodle and Prawn Aglio Olio with chopped fresh parsley and grated Parmesan cheese.

Nutritional Values (per serving, assuming 2 servings, without optional garnishes): Calories: 300 Kcal; Protein: 18g; Carbohydrates: 10g; Fat: 21g

Beef Lettuce Wraps with Cucumber Slaw

Time: 30 minutes
Preparation: 20 minutes
Cooking: 10 minutes
Servings: 4

INGREDIENTS

- For the Beef Lettuce Wraps:
- 1 pound ground beef
- 1 small onion, finely diced
- 2 cloves garlic, minced
- 1 tablespoon ginger, minced
- 1/4 cup soy sauce (or tamari for a gluten-free option)
- 1 tablespoon sesame oil
- 1 tablespoon rice vinegar
- 1 teaspoon honey or a sugar-free sweetener
- 1/4 cup green onions, chopped
- Salt and black pepper to taste
- 1 head of iceberg or Romaine lettuce, separated into leaves
- For the Cucumber Slaw:
- 1 cucumber, julienned
- 1 carrot, julienned

- 1/4 cup rice vinegar
- 1 tablespoon honey or a sugar-free sweetener
- 1 teaspoon sesame seeds (optional)
- Salt and black pepper to taste

INSTRUCTIONS

Beef Lettuce Wraps:
1. Sauté Beef and Aromatics:
   - In a large skillet, brown the ground beef over medium-high heat.
   - Add the minced garlic, minced ginger, and diced onion. Sauté for a few minutes until the onions are translucent and the beef is cooked through.
2. Prepare the Sauce:
   - In a small bowl, whisk together the soy sauce, sesame oil, rice vinegar, honey, chopped green onions, salt, and black pepper.
3. Combine Beef and Sauce:
   - Pour the sauce over the cooked beef mixture. Stir to coat the beef evenly. Let it simmer for a few minutes.
4. Serve in Lettuce Cups:
   - Carefully separate the lettuce leaves and wash them.
   - To make wraps, spoon the beef mixture into the lettuce leaves.

Cucumber Slaw:
1. Prepare the Slaw:
   - In a mixing bowl, combine the julienned cucumber and carrot.
2. Make the Dressing:
   - In a separate bowl, whisk together the rice vinegar, honey, sesame seeds (if desired), salt, and black pepper.
3. Toss and Serve:
   - Pour the dressing over the cucumber and carrot mixture.
   - Allow the slaw to marinade for a few minutes after tossing to coat.

Serve the Wraps and Slaw:
- Serve the Beef Lettuce Wraps with Cucumber Slaw on the side, allowing diners to add slaw to their wraps as desired.

Nutritional Values (per serving, assuming 4 servings, without optional garnishes): Calories: 250 Kcal; Protein: 15g; Carbohydrates: 12g; Fat: 16g

Asparagus and Goat Cheese Quiche

Time: 1 hour
Preparation: 15 minutes
Cooking: 45 minutes
Servings: 6

INGREDIENTS

- For the Quiche Filling:
- 1 bunch of asparagus, tough ends removed and cut into 1-inch pieces
- 1 cup goat cheese, crumbled
- 4 large eggs
- 1 cup heavy cream
- 1/4 cup fresh chives, chopped
- Salt and black pepper to taste
- For the Quiche Crust:
- 1 1/4 cups almond flour
- 1/4 cup obutter, melted
- 1 egg
- 1/4 teaspoon salt

INSTRUCTIONS

Quiche Crust:

1. Preheat Oven:
   - Set the oven temperature to 175°C, or 350°F.
2. Prepare Crust:
   - In a mixing bowl, combine the almond flour, melted butter, egg, and salt.
   - Stir until the ingredients combine to create a dough.
3. Press into Pan:
   - Press the dough into the bottom of a 9-inch tart or quiche pan, forming an even crust.
4. Bake Crust:
   - Place the crust in the preheated oven and bake for 10-12 minutes or until it's lightly golden.
5. Remove and Cool:
   - Remove the crust from the oven and allow it to cool while you prepare the filling.

Quiche Filling:

1. Blanch Asparagus:
   - In a pot of boiling water, blanch the asparagus for 2-3 minutes until they are tender but still crisp.
   - Drain and transfer them to a bowl of ice water to stop the cooking process.
2. Whisk Eggs and Cream:
   - In a separate bowl, whisk together the eggs and heavy cream. Season with salt and black pepper.
3. Assemble Quiche:
   - Sprinkle the crumbled goat cheese over the baked crust.
   - Arrange the blanched asparagus on top..
   - Drizzle the asparagus and cheese with the egg and cream mixture.
4. Bake Quiche:
   - Place the quiche in the preheated oven and bake for about 35-40 minutes, or until the quiche is set and the top is lightly browned.
5. Cool and Serve:
   - Allow the quiche to cool slightly before slicing and serving.
   - Garnish with chopped fresh chives.

Nutritional Values (per serving, assuming 6 servings): Calories: 380 Kcal; Protein: 12g; Carbohydrates: 7g; Fat: 34g

Seared Tuna Salad with Mixed Greens

Time: 20 minutes
Preparation: 15 minutes
Cooking: 5 minutes
Servings: 2

INGREDIENTS

- For the Seared Tuna:
- 2 tuna steaks (about 6 ounces each)
- 1 tablespoon olive oil
- Salt and black pepper to taste
- 1 tablespoon sesame seeds
- 1 teaspoon soy sauce (or tamari for a gluten-free option)
- For the Salad:
- 6 cups mixed salad greens (e.g., arugula, spinach, and romaine)
- 1 cup cherry tomatoes, halved
- 1/2 cup cucumber, sliced
- 1/4 cup red onion, thinly sliced
- 2 hard-boiled eggs, sliced
- For the Vinaigrette:

- 3 tablespoons extra-virgin olive oil
- 1 tablespoon balsamic vinegar
- 1 clove garlic, minced
- 1/2 teaspoon Dijon mustard
- Salt and black pepper to taste

INSTRUCTIONS

Seared Tuna:
1. Season Tuna:
   - Season the tuna steaks with salt and black pepper.
2. Sear Tuna:
   - Heat 1 tablespoon of olive oil in a skillet over high heat.
   - Sear the tuna steaks for about 1-2 minutes per side for rare or longer if desired.
   - Brush the tops of the seared tuna steaks with soy sauce and then coat them with sesame seeds.
3. Slice Tuna:
   - Allow the tuna to rest for a few minutes, then slice it into thin strips.

Vinaigrette:
1. Prepare Vinaigrette:
   - Combine the extra-virgin olive oil, balsamic vinegar, Dijon mustard, minced garlic, salt, and black pepper in a small bowl. To suit your taste.

Salad:
1. Assemble Salad:
   - In a large salad bowl, combine the mixed salad greens, cherry tomatoes, cucumber, red onion, and hard-boiled egg slices.
2. Dress Salad:
   - Drizzle the vinaigrette over the salad and toss to combine.

Serve:
- Divide the dressed salad into two plates.
- Top each salad with the sliced seared tuna.

Nutritional Values (per serving, assuming 2 servings): Calories: 350 Kcal; Protein: 30g; Carbohydrates: 10g; Fat: 20g

Lamb Kofta with Tzatziki Sauce

Time: 30 minutes
Preparation: 15 minutes
Cooking: 15 minutes
Servings: 4

INGREDIENTS
- For the Lamb Kofta:
- 1 pound ground lamb
- 1/2 red onion, finely grated
- 2 cloves garlic, minced
- 1 teaspoon ground cumin
- 1 teaspoon ground coriander
- 1/2 teaspoon ground cinnamon
- 1/4 cup fresh parsley, chopped
- Salt and black pepper to taste
- Wooden skewers, soaked in water for 30 minutes
- For the Tzatziki Sauce:
- 1 cup Greek yogurt
- 1/2 cucumber, finely grated and drained
- 2 cloves garlic, minced
- 1 tablespoon fresh dill, chopped
- 1 tablespoon lemon juice
- 1 tablespoon extra-virgin olive oil
- Salt and black pepper to taste

INSTRUCTIONS

Lamb Kofta:
1. Prepare Skewers:
   - Preheat your grill or grill pan to medium-high heat.
   - Thread the soaked wooden skewers through the ground lamb mixture to form kofta shapes.
2. Season and Grill:
   - Season the lamb kofta with salt and black pepper.
   - Grill the kofta for about 6-8 minutes, turning occasionally, until they are cooked to your desired level of doneness.

Tzatziki Sauce:
1. Prepare Tzatziki:
   - In a bowl, combine the Greek yogurt, finely grated and drained cucumber, minced garlic,

chopped fresh dill, lemon juice, olive oil, salt, and black pepper.
- Mix until well combined.

2. Chill Tzatziki:
- Cover the Tzatziki sauce and refrigerate it until you're ready to serve.

Serve:
- Serve the Lamb Kofta hot off the grill with a side of the chilled Tzatziki sauce.

Nutritional Values (per serving, assuming 4 servings): Calories: 380 Kcal; Protein: 20g; Carbohydrates: 5g; Fat: 30g

Coconut Milk and Chicken Curry Soup

Time: 45 minutes
Preparation: 15 minutes
Cooking: 30 minutes
Servings: 4

INGREDIENTS

- For the Soup:
- 2 chicken breasts, boneless and skinless, cut into bite-sized pieces
- 1 tablespoon coconut oil
- 1 small onion, finely chopped
- 2 cloves garlic, minced
- 1 tablespoon ginger, minced
- 2 tablespoons red curry paste
- 4 cups chicken broth (low-sodium)
- 1 can (14 ounces) coconut milk
- 1 red bell pepper, thinly sliced
- 1 cup broccoli florets
- 1 cup snap peas, trimmed
- Juice of 1 lime
- Salt and black pepper to taste
- Fresh cilantro for garnish

INSTRUCTIONS

1. Sauté Chicken:
- In a large pot, heat the coconut oil over medium-high heat.
- Add the chicken pieces and cook until they are no longer pink. Remove the cooked chicken from the pot and set it aside.

2. Sauté Aromatics:
- Add the chopped onion to the same saucepan and sauté it for about 3 minutes, or until it turns translucent.
  - Add the minced garlic and ginger. Sauté for another minute until fragrant.

3. Add Curry Paste:
- Stir in the red curry paste and cook for about 2 minutes, stirring to combine it with the aromatics.

4. Combine Broth and Coconut Milk:
- Pour in the chicken broth and the coconut milk. Stir well to combine all the ingredients in the pot.

5. Simmer Soup:
- Bring the soup to a gentle simmer. Let it cook for about 10 minutes.

6. Add Vegetables:
- Add the sliced red bell pepper, broccoli florets, and snap peas to the pot. Continue to simmer for another 10 minutes or until the vegetables are tender but still crisp.

7. Return Chicken:
- Return the cooked chicken pieces to the pot.

8. Season and Finish:
- Squeeze the juice of 1 lime into the soup.
  - To taste, add salt and black pepper for seasoning. Adjust the seasonings to your preference.

9. Garnish and Serve:
- Ladle the Coconut Milk and Chicken Curry Soup into bowls.
- Garnish with fresh cilantro leaves before serving.

Nutritional Values (per serving, assuming 4 servings): Calories: 350 Kcal; Protein: 30g; Carbohydrates: 12g; Fat: 20g

Spinach and Walnut Stuffed Chicken Breast

Time: 45 minutes
Preparation: 20 minutes
Cooking: 25 minutes
Servings: 4

INGREDIENTS

- For the Stuffed Chicken:

- 4 boneless, skinless chicken breasts
- 2 cups fresh spinach, chopped
- 1/2 cup walnuts, finely chopped
- 1/2 cup feta cheese, crumbled
- 1 clove garlic, minced
- 2 tablespoons olive oil
- Salt and black pepper to taste
- Toothpicks or kitchen twine (for securing the chicken)
- For the Sauce:
- 1/2 cup chicken broth
- 1/4 cup heavy cream
- 1 tablespoon Dijon mustard
- 1 tablespoon fresh lemon juice
- 1 tablespoon fresh parsley, chopped
- Salt and black pepper to taste

INSTRUCTIONS

Stuffed Chicken:
1. Preheat Oven:
   - Preheat your oven to 375°F (190°C).
2. Prepare Chicken:
   - Place each chicken breast between two sheets of plastic wrap and gently pound them to an even thickness, about 1/2 inch thick.
3. Prepare Stuffing:
   - In a bowl, combine the chopped spinach, finely chopped walnuts, crumbled feta cheese, minced garlic, olive oil, salt, and black pepper.
4. Stuff Chicken:
   - Spoon the spinach and walnut mixture onto one side of each chicken breast.
   - Carefully fold the other side of the chicken breast over the filling.
5. Secure Chicken:
   - Secure the stuffed chicken breasts with toothpicks or kitchen twine to keep the filling in place.
6. Sear Chicken:
   - In an oven-safe skillet, heat some olive oil over medium-high heat.
   - Sear the stuffed chicken breasts for about 2-3 minutes per side until they are browned.
7. Finish in Oven:
   - Transfer the skillet to the preheated oven and bake for about 15-20 minutes or until the chicken is cooked through (internal temperature of 165°F or 74°C).

Sauce:
1. Prepare Sauce:
   - In a separate saucepan, combine the chicken broth, heavy cream, Dijon mustard, and lemon juice.
   - Heat the sauce over medium heat until it thickens, stirring frequently.
   - To taste, add salt and black pepper for seasoning.

Serve:
- Remove the toothpicks or kitchen twine from the chicken breasts.
- Serve the stuffed chicken breasts drizzled with the creamy Dijon sauce.
- Garnish with chopped fresh parsley.

Nutritional Values (per serving, assuming 4 servings): Calories: 400 Kcal; Protein: 40g; Carbohydrates: 6g; Fat: 25g

Pork Stir-fry with Bell Peppers

Time: 30 minutes
Preparation: 15 minutes
Cooking: 15 minutes
Servings: 4

INGREDIENTS

- For the Stir-fry:
- 1 pound pork tenderloin, thinly sliced
- 2 bell peppers (assorted colors), thinly sliced
- 1 red onion, thinly sliced
- 2 cloves garlic, minced
- 1 tablespoon ginger, minced
- 2 tablespoons coconut oil or vegetable oil
- Salt and black pepper to taste
- Fresh cilantro for garnish (optional)
- For the Stir-fry Sauce:
- 1/4 cup soy sauce (or tamari for a gluten-free option)
- 2 tablespoons rice vinegar
- 1 tablespoon honey or a sugar-free sweetener
- 1 teaspoon sesame oil
- 1/2 teaspoon red pepper flakes (adjust to taste)

INSTRUCTIONS

Stir-fry Sauce:

1. Prepare the Sauce:
   - In a small bowl, whisk together the soy sauce, rice vinegar, honey, sesame oil, and red pepper flakes to make the stir-fry sauce. Set it aside.

Stir-fry:

1. Marinate Pork:
   - In a bowl, combine the sliced pork with half of the stir-fry sauce. Allow it to marinate for about 10 minutes.
2. Heat Oil:
   - In a large skillet or wok, heat the coconut oil or vegetable oil over high heat.
3. Sear Pork:
   - Add the marinated pork to the hot skillet and stir-fry for 3-4 minutes until it's browned and cooked through. Remove it from the skillet and set it aside.
4. Sauté Aromatics and Veggies:
   - In the same skillet, add the minced garlic and ginger. Sauté for about 1 minute until fragrant.
   - Add the sliced bell peppers and red onion. Stir-fry for about 5 minutes until they are tender-crisp.
5. Combine and Simmer:
   - Return the cooked pork to the skillet with the sautéed vegetables.
   - Pour the remaining stir-fry sauce over the pork and vegetables.
   - Simmer for a few minutes until everything is heated through and coated with the sauce.
6. Serve:
   - Serve your Pork Stir-fry with Bell Peppers hot, garnished with fresh cilantro if desired.

Nutritional Values (per serving, assuming 4 servings): Calories: 300 Kcal; Protein: 25g; Carbohydrates: 15g; Fat: 15g

Shrimp Avocado Salad with Lemon Dressing

Time: 20 minutes
Preparation: 15 minutes
Cooking: 5 minutes
Servings: 4

INGREDIENTS

- For the Salad:
- 1 pound large shrimp, peeled and deveined
- 4 cups mixed salad greens (e.g., arugula, spinach, and romaine)
- 2 avocados, peeled, pitted, and sliced
- 1/2 cup cherry tomatoes, halved
- 1/4 cup red onion, thinly sliced
- 1/4 cup cucumber, sliced
- Fresh cilantro for garnish (optional)
- For the Lemon Dressing:
- 1/4 cup extra-virgin olive oil
- Juice of 2 lemons
- 1 clove garlic, minced
- 1 teaspoon honey or a sugar-free sweetener (adjust to taste)
- Salt and black pepper to taste

INSTRUCTIONS

Salad:

1. Sear Shrimp:
   - Heat a skillet over medium-high heat.
   - Sear the shrimp for about 2-3 minutes per side until they turn pink and are cooked through.
2. Prepare Salad Greens:
   - In a large salad bowl, combine the mixed greens, sliced avocados, cherry tomatoes, red onion, and cucumber.

Lemon Dressing:

1. Prepare Dressing:
   - To prepare the lemon dressing, combine the extra-virgin olive oil, lemon juice, minced garlic, honey, salt, and black pepper in a small bowl.

Combine and Serve:

1. Combine Salad and Shrimp:
   - Add the seared shrimp to the salad.

2. Dress Salad:
   - Drizzle the lemon dressing over the salad and shrimp.
3. Toss and Serve:
   - Gently toss the salad to distribute the dressing evenly among the components.
4. Garnish and Serve:
   - Optionally, garnish with fresh cilantro leaves before serving.

Nutritional Values (per serving, assuming 4 servings): Calories: 300 Kcal; Protein: 20g; Carbohydrates: 14g; Fat: 20g

Grilled Eggplant and Zucchini Stacks with Mozzarella

Time: 45 minutes
Preparation: 15 minutes
Cooking: 30 minutes
Servings: 4

INGREDIENTS

- For the Grilled Vegetables:
- 1 eggplant, sliced into 1/4-inch rounds
- 2 zucchinis, sliced into 1/4-inch rounds
- 2 tablespoons extra-virgin olive oil
- Salt and black pepper to taste
- For the Tomato Sauce:
- 1 cup tomato sauce
- 1 clove garlic, minced
- 1 teaspoon fresh basil, chopped
- Salt and black pepper to taste
- For the Stacks:
- 8 fresh mozzarella slices
- Fresh basil leaves
- Grated Parmesan cheese (for garnish, optional)

INSTRUCTIONS

Grilled Vegetables:
1. Preheat Grill:
   - Set your grill's temperature to medium-high.
2. Prepare Vegetables:
   - Brush the eggplant and zucchini slices with olive oil and season with salt and black pepper.

3. Grill Vegetables:
   - Grill the eggplant and zucchini slices for about 2-3 minutes per side or until they are tender and have grill marks.

Tomato Sauce:
1. Prepare Sauce:
   - In a small saucepan, combine the tomato sauce, minced garlic, chopped basil, salt, and black pepper.
   - Heat the sauce over low heat for a few minutes until it's warmed through.

Stacks:
1. Assemble Stacks:
   - To create each stack, start with a slice of grilled eggplant.
   - Add a slice of grilled zucchini on top.
   - Add a fresh mozzarella slice and a basil leaf.
   - Repeat the layers to create a stack.
2. Warm Stacks:
   - Place the stacks on the grill for 2-3 minutes or until the mozzarella begins to melt.

Serve:
   - Drizzle the tomato sauce over the Grilled Eggplant and Zucchini Stacks with Mozzarella.
   - You can choose to add grated Parmesan cheese as a garnish.

Nutritional Values (per serving, assuming 4 servings, without optional garnishes): Calories: 250 Kcal; Protein: 10g; Carbohydrates: 15g; Fat: 15g

Greek Salad with Olives and Feta

Time: 15 minutes
Preparation: 15 minutes
Servings: 4

INGREDIENTS

- For the Salad:
- 4 cups cucumbers, diced
- 4 cups tomatoes, diced
- 1 cup red onion, thinly sliced
- 1 cup Kalamata olives, pitted
- 1 cup feta cheese, crumbled
- 1/4 cup fresh parsley, chopped

- 1/4 cup fresh mint, chopped (optional)
- Salt and black pepper to taste
- For the Greek Salad Dressing:
- 1/4 cup extra-virgin olive oil
- 2 tablespoons red wine vinegar
- 1 clove garlic, minced
- 1 teaspoon dried oregano
- Salt and black pepper to taste

INSTRUCTIONS

Salad:
1. Prepare Vegetables:
   - In a large salad bowl, combine the diced cucumbers, diced tomatoes, sliced red onion, and Kalamata olives.
2. Add Feta and Herbs:
   - Gently fold in the crumbled feta cheese, chopped fresh parsley, and mint (if using).

Greek Salad Dressing:
1. Prepare Dressing:
   - To create the Greek salad dressing, combine the extra virgin olive oil, red wine vinegar, minced garlic, dried oregano, salt, and black pepper in a small bowl.

Serve:
- Drizzle the Greek Salad Dressing over the salad.
- Gently toss the salad to combine all the ingredients and coat them with the dressing.

Nutritional Values (per serving, assuming 4 servings): Calories: 280 Kcal; Protein: 8g; Carbohydrates: 12g; Fat: 23g

Chard and Bacon Wrapped Scallops

Time: 30 minutes
Preparation: 15 minutes
Cooking: 15 minutes
Servings: 4

INGREDIENTS

- For the Scallops:
- 12 large sea scallops
- 12 slices bacon
- Salt and black pepper to taste

- Toothpicks or wooden skewers (soaked in water)
- For the Chard:
- 8 cups chard leaves, stems removed and chopped
- 2 cloves garlic, minced
- 2 tablespoons olive oil
- Salt and black pepper to taste

INSTRUCTIONS

Chard:
1. Sauté Chard:
   - Heat olive oil in a big skillet over medium heat.
   - Add the minced garlic and sauté for about 30 seconds until fragrant.
   - When the chard leaves are soft and wilted, add them and sauté them for 5 to 7 minutes.
   - To taste, add salt and black pepper for seasoning.. Set aside.

Scallops:
1. Prepare Scallops:
   - Use a paper towel to pat the scallops dry.
   - Season them with salt and black pepper.
2. Wrap Scallops:
   - Using a toothpick or skewer, enclose each scallop with a slice of bacon.
3. Sear Scallops:
   - Sear the scallops wrapped in bacon in a skillet over medium-high heat for two to three minutes on each side, or until the bacon is crisp and the scallops are cooked through.

Serve:
- Serve the Chard and Bacon Wrapped Scallops over the sautéed chard.
- Optionally, garnish with fresh herbs or a squeeze of lemon juice.

Nutritional Values (per serving, assuming 4 servings): Calories: 300 Kcal; Protein: 25g; Carbohydrates: 5g; Fat: 20g

Cauliflower Fried Rice with Chicken

Time: 30 minutes
Preparation: 15 minutes
Cooking: 15 minutes
Servings: 4

INGREDIENTS

- For the Fried Rice:
- 1 large head of cauliflower, riced (use a food processor or box grater)
- 2 chicken breasts, diced into bite-sized pieces
- 2 eggs, lightly beaten
- 1/2 cup peas (fresh or frozen)
- 1/2 cup carrots, diced
- 1/2 cup red bell pepper, diced
- 1/2 cup green onions, chopped
- 2 cloves garlic, minced
- 2 tablespoons sesame oil
- 2 tablespoons coconut aminos (or soy sauce)
- 2 tablespoons olive oil
- Salt and black pepper to taste

INSTRUCTIONS

Fried Rice:
1. Prepare Chicken:
   - In a large skillet or wok, heat 1 tablespoon of olive oil over medium-high heat.
   - Add the diced chicken and cook it through, making sure it's no longer pink. After removing it from the skillet, set the chicken aside.
2. Scramble Eggs:
   - In the same skillet, add the beaten eggs. Eggs should be scrambled until done but still somewhat runny. Take them out of the skillet and place it aside.
3. Stir-fry Veggies:
   - Fill the skillet with the final tablespoon of olive oil.
   - Add the garlic, diced carrots, and red bell pepper. Stir-fry the veggies for two to three minutes, or until they begin to soften.
4. Add Cauliflower Rice:
   - Add the riced cauliflower and simmer, stirring occasionally, until the cauliflower is soft and beginning to brown, about 5 to 7 minutes.
5. Combine Ingredients:
   - Fill the skillet with the cooked chicken, chopped green onions, peas, and scrambled eggs. Mix everything thoroughly.
6. Season:
   - Drizzle the sesame oil and coconut aminos (or soy sauce) over the cauliflower fried
   - To taste, add salt and black pepper for seasoning.
7. Stir-fry:
   - Stir-fry for an additional two to three minutes, or until well heated.

Serve:
- Serve your Cauliflower Fried Rice with Chicken hot.
- Optionally, garnish with additional green onions.

Nutritional Values (per serving, assuming 4 servings): Calories: 300 Kcal; Protein: 25g; Carbohydrates: 10g; Fat: 15g

Beef and Vegetable Kebabs

Time: 30 minutes (plus marinating time)
Preparation: 15 minutes
Cooking: 15 minutes
Servings: 4

INGREDIENTS

- For the Beef Marinade:
- 1 pound beef sirloin or tenderloin, cut into 1-inch cubes
- 2 tablespoons olive oil
- 2 cloves garlic, minced
- 1 teaspoon dried oregano
- 1 teaspoon paprika
- Salt and black pepper to taste
- For the Kebabs:
- 2 red bell peppers, cut into 1-inch pieces
- 2 yellow bell peppers, cut into 1-inch pieces
- 1 red onion, cut into 1-inch pieces
- 8 cremini or button mushrooms
- Wooden skewers, soaked in water for 30 minutes

INSTRUCTIONS

Beef Marinade:

1. Prepare Marinade:
   - In a bowl, combine the olive oil, minced garlic, dried oregano, paprika, salt, and black pepper to make the beef marinade.
2. Marinate Beef:
   - Make sure the meat cubes are thoroughly covered by tossing them in the marinade.
   - Cover and refrigerate for at least 30 minutes, allowing the flavors to meld.

Kebabs:

1. Prepare Skewers:
   - Set your grill's temperature to medium-high.
2. Assemble Kebabs:
   - Thread the marinated beef, red bell peppers, yellow bell peppers, red onion, and mushrooms onto the soaked wooden skewers, alternating ingredients.
3. Grill Kebabs:
   - Cook the beef and vegetable kebabs on the grill for ten to fifteen minutes, flipping them from time to time, until the steak is cooked through and the veggies are soft and gently browned.
4. Serve:
   - Serve your Beef and Vegetable Kebabs hot off the grill.

Nutritional Values (per serving, assuming 4 servings): Calories: 300 Kcal; Protein: 25g; Carbohydrates: 10g; Fat: 15g

Herb Roasted Chicken with Brussels Sprouts

Time: 1 hour
Preparation: 15 minutes
Cooking: 45 minutes
Servings: 4

INGREDIENTS

- For the Herb Roasted Chicken:
- 4 chicken leg quarters (drumsticks and thighs)
- 2 tablespoons olive oil
- 2 tablespoons fresh rosemary, chopped
- 2 tablespoons fresh thyme, chopped
- 2 cloves garlic, minced
- Salt and black pepper to taste
- 1 o lemon, sliced into rounds
- For the Brussels Sprouts:
- 1 pound Brussels sprouts, trimmed and halved
- 2 tablespoons olive oil
- Salt and black pepper to taste

INSTRUCTIONS

Herb Roasted Chicken:
1. Preheat Oven:
   - Preheat your oven to 425°F (220°C).
2. Prepare Chicken:
   - Use paper towels to pat the chicken leg quarters dry
   - Olive oil, minced garlic, chopped thyme, chopped rosemary, salt, and black pepper should all be combined in a bowl.
3. Marinate Chicken:
   - Rub the herb mixture all over the chicken pieces.
   - Top each piece of chicken with a slice of lemon.
4. Roast Chicken:
   - Place the quartered chicken legs on a roasting pan or baking sheet.
   - Roast for 35 to 45 minutes, or until the chicken is thoroughly cooked and the skin is crispy, in a preheated oven.

Brussels Sprouts:
1. Prepare Brussels Sprouts:
   - Toss the halved Brussels sprouts with black pepper, salt, and olive oil in a another bowl.

2. Roast Brussels Sprouts:
   - During the last 20-25 minutes of the chicken's cooking time, add the seasoned Brussels sprouts to the baking sheet or roasting pan with the chicken.
   - Roast the Brussels sprouts until they become soft and have a hint of colour..

Serve:
   - If preferred, top your hot Herb Roasted Chicken with Brussels Sprouts with fresh herbs.

Nutritional Values (per serving, assuming 4 servings): Calories: 400 Kcal; Protein: 30g; Carbohydrates: 10g; Fat: 25g

Lamb Chops with Mint Pesto and Asparagus

Time: 30 minutes
Preparation: 15 minutes
Cooking: 15 minutes
Servings: 4

INGREDIENTS

- For the Lamb Chops:
- 8 lamb chops (about 2 pounds)
- 2 tablespoons olive oil
- Salt and black pepper to taste
- For the Mint Pesto:
- 1 cup fresh mint leaves
- 1/2 cup fresh parsley leaves
- 1/4 cup almonds, toasted
- 2 cloves garlic, minced
- 1/2 cup extra-virgin olive oil
- 1/4 cup grated Parmesan cheese
- Juice of 1 lemon
- Salt and black pepper to taste
- For the Asparagus:
- 1 pound asparagus, trimmed
- 2 tablespoons olive oil
- Salt and black pepper to taste

INSTRUCTIONS

Lamb Chops:
1. Preheat Grill or Pan:
   - Preheat your grill or a grill pan over medium-high heat.

2. Prepare Lamb Chops:
   - Brush the lamb chops with olive oil and season them with salt and black pepper.
3. Grill Lamb Chops:
   - Grill the lamb chops for about 3-4 minutes per side for medium-rare (adjust cooking time to your desired doneness).
   - Take them off the grill and give them a few minutes to rest.

Mint Pesto:
1. Prepare Pesto:
   - In a food processor, combine the fresh mint leaves, fresh parsley leaves, toasted almonds, minced garlic, extra-virgin olive oil, grated Parmesan cheese, and lemon juice.
   - Pulse until the consistency of the pesto is smooth.

Asparagus:
1. Prepare Asparagus:
   - Toss the trimmed asparagus with olive oil, salt, and black pepper.
2. Grill Asparagus:
   - Grill the asparagus on the same grill for about 2-3 minutes until they are tender and slightly charred.

Serve:
   - Serve your Lamb Chops with a drizzle of Mint Pesto and a side of grilled asparagus.

Nutritional Values (per serving, assuming 4 servings): Calories: 400 Kcal; Protein: 35g; Carbohydrates: 8g; Fat: 25g

Cauliflower Pizza with Cheese and Veggies

Time: 45 minutes
Preparation: 15 minutes
Cooking: 30 minutes
Servings: 4

INGREDIENTS

- For the Cauliflower Crust:
- 1 large head of cauliflower, riced (use a food processor)
- 1 egg
- 1/2 cup mozzarella cheese, shredded
- 1/2 teaspoon dried oregano

- 1/2 teaspoon garlic powder
- Salt and black pepper to taste
- For the Pizza Toppings:
- 1/2 cup omato sauce
- 1 cup omozzarella cheese, shredded
- 1 red bell pepper, thinly sliced
- 1 yellow bell pepper, thinly sliced
- 1 red onion, thinly sliced
- 1 cup baby spinach
- 1/2 cup cherry tomatoes, halved
- Fresh basil leaves for garnish (optional)
- Red pepper flakes (optional)

INSTRUCTIONS

Cauliflower Crust:

1. Preheat Oven:
   - Preheat your oven to 425°F (220°C).
2. Prepare Cauliflower Crust:
   - Rice the cauliflower in a food processor, and then transfer it to a clean kitchen towel.
   - Squeeze out excess moisture from the cauliflower.
3. Combine Ingredients:
   - In a bowl, combine the riced cauliflower, egg, 1/2 cup mozzarella cheese, dried oregano, garlic powder, salt, and black pepper.
4. Bake Crust:
   - Press the cauliflower mixture onto a parchment paper-lined baking sheet to form a pizza crust.
   - Bake for 15 to 20 minutes, or until brown and firm, in the preheated oven.

Pizza:

1. Prepare Pizza Toppings:
   - Spread the tomato sauce over the cauliflower crust, leaving a border for the crust.
2. Add Veggies and Cheese:
   - Sprinkle the shredded mozzarella cheese over the tomato sauce.
   - Place the cherry tomatoes, red onion, and sliced yellow and orange bell peppers on top.
3. Bake Pizza:
   - Return the pizza to the oven and bake for another 10-12 minutes or until the cheese is melted and bubbly.
4. Add Greens:
   - Just before serving, scatter baby spinach over the hot pizza, allowing it to wilt slightly.

Garnish:

- Optionally, garnish your Cauliflower Pizza with fresh basil leaves and red pepper flakes.

Nutritional Values (per serving, assuming 4 servings): Calories: 250 Kcal; Protein: 12g; Carbohydrates: 15g; Fat: 15g

Thai Coconut Fish Curry with Zucchini Noodles

Time: 30 minutes
Preparation: 15 minutes
Cooking: 15 minutes
Servings: 4

INGREDIENTS

- For the Curry:
- 1 pound white fish fillets (such as cod or tilapia), cut into bite-sized pieces
- 2 tablespoons coconut oil
- 1 onion, finely chopped
- 2 cloves garlic, minced
- 1 tablespoon fresh ginger, minced
- 2 tablespoons Thai red curry paste
- 1 can (14 oz) coconut milk
- 1 cup cherry tomatoes, halved
- 1 red bell pepper, sliced
- 1 zucchini, spiralized into noodles
- Juice of 1 lime
- Salt and black pepper to taste
- Fresh cilantro leaves for garnish

INSTRUCTIONS

Curry:

1. Sauté Onion:
   - In a large skillet or wok, heat the coconut oil over medium-high heat.
   - When the onion is transparent, add the finely chopped onion and sauté it.
2. Add Garlic and Ginger:
   - Stir in the minced garlic and ginger and cook for about 1-2 minutes until fragrant.
3. Add Curry Paste:
   - Add the Thai red curry paste to the skillet and cook for 2-3 minutes, stirring to incorporate.

4. Coconut Milk:
   - Pour in the coconut milk and stir well.
5. Simmer Curry:
   - Allow the curry to simmer for about 5 minutes or until it thickens slightly.
6. Add Tomatoes and Bell Pepper:
   - Add the halved cherry tomatoes and sliced red bell pepper. Simmer them for a further two to three minutes to make them softer.

Fish and Zucchini Noodles:
1. Cook Fish:
   - Gently add the fish fillets to the simmering curry. Cook until the salmon is done, about 5 minutes.
2. Zucchini Noodles:
   - Just before serving, add the spiralized zucchini noodles to the curry and cook for 2-3 minutes until they are tender but still crisp.
3. Lime Juice and Season:
   - Squeeze the juice of one lime into the curry.
   - To taste, add salt and black pepper for seasoning.

Serve:
   - Serve your Thai Coconut Fish Curry with Zucchini Noodles.
   - Optionally, garnish with fresh cilantro leaves.

Nutritional Values (per serving, assuming 4 servings): Calories: 300 Kcal; Protein: 25g; Carbohydrates: 10g; Fat: 18g

Pork Ribs with Kale Slaw

Time: 3 hours
Preparation: 15 minutes
Cooking: 2 hours and 45 minutes
Servings: 4

INGREDIENTS

- For the Pork Ribs:
- 2 racks of pork ribs
- 2 tablespoons olive oil
- 2 tablespoons paprika
- 1 tablespoon garlic powder
- 1 tablespoon onion powder
- 1 teaspoon cayenne pepper (adjust to your spice preference)
- Salt and black pepper to taste

- 2 cups barbecue sauce
- For the Kale Slaw:
- 4 cups kale, stems removed and finely chopped
- 1 cup red cabbage, thinly sliced
- 1 cup carrots, shredded
- 1/2 cup mayonnaise
- 2 tablespoons apple cider vinegar
- 1 tablespoon Dijon mustard
- 1 tablespoon honey
- Salt and black pepper to taste

INSTRUCTIONS

Pork Ribs:
1. Preheat Oven:
   - Preheat your oven to 300°F (150°C).
2. Prepare Ribs:
   - Remove the membrane from the back of the pork ribs.
   - In a bowl, combine the olive oil, paprika, garlic powder, onion powder, cayenne pepper, salt, and black pepper.
3. Rub Ribs:
   - Rub the spice mixture all over the pork ribs.
4. Wrap and Bake:
   - Wrap each rack of ribs in aluminum foil, creating a tight seal.
   - Place the wrapped ribs on a baking sheet and bake in the preheated oven for about 2.5 hours or until they are tender.
5. Grill Ribs:
   - Set your grill's temperature to medium-high.
   - After taking the ribs out of the oven, carefully unwrap them..
   - Grill the ribs for about 10-15 minutes, basting with barbecue sauce, until they develop a nice char and are heated through.

Kale Slaw:
1. Prepare Slaw:
   - In a large bowl, combine the finely chopped kale, sliced red cabbage, and shredded carrots.
2. Prepare Dressing:
   - In a separate bowl, whisk together the mayonnaise, apple cider vinegar, Dijon mustard, honey, salt, and black pepper to create the dressing.
3. Toss and Chill:
   - Drizzle the dressing over the kale slaw and toss to coat evenly.

- Before serving, let the slaw sit in the fridge for at least half an hour.

Serve:
- Serve your Pork Ribs with a side of Kale Slaw.

Nutritional Values (per serving, assuming 4 servings, without extra barbecue sauce): Calories: 700 Kcal; Protein: 25g; Carbohydrates: 15g; Fat: 50g

Garlic Butter Shrimp with Broccoli Rice

Time: 30 minutes
Preparation: 15 minutes
Cooking: 15 minutes Servings: 4

INGREDIENTS

- For the Garlic Butter Shrimp:
- 1 pound large shrimp, peeled and deveined
- 4 tablespoons butter
- 4 cloves garlic, minced
- 1 tablespoon fresh parsley, chopped
- Juice of 1 lemon
- Salt and black pepper to taste
- For the Broccoli Rice:
- 4 cups broccoli florets
- 2 tablespoons olive oil
- Salt and black pepper to taste

INSTRUCTIONS

Garlic Butter Shrimp:
1. Prepare Shrimp:
   - Season the peeled and deveined shrimp with salt and black pepper.
2. Cook Shrimp:
   - In a large skillet, melt 2 tablespoons of butter over medium-high heat.
   - When the garlic is aromatic, add the minced garlic and sauté for about one minute.
   - Add the seasoned shrimp to the skillet and cook for 2-3 minutes per side until they turn pink and opaque.
3. Finish with Lemon and Parsley:
   - Squeeze the juice of one lemon over the cooked shrimp.

- Add chopped fresh parsley and the remaining 2 tablespoons of butter.
- Toss everything together until the shrimp are coated in garlic butter sauce. Set aside.

Broccoli Rice:
1. Prepare Broccoli Rice:
   - In a food processor, pulse the broccoli florets until they reach a rice-like consistency.
2. Sauté Broccoli Rice:
   - In a separate skillet, heat the olive oil over medium heat.
   - Add the riced broccoli and sauté for 4-5 minutes until it's tender and slightly crisp.
   - Season with salt and black pepper.

Serve:
- Serve your Garlic Butter Shrimp over the sautéed Broccoli Rice.

Nutritional Values (per serving, assuming 4 servings): Calories: 250 Kcal; Protein: 25g; Carbohydrates: 5g; Fat: 15g

Grilled Steak with Chimichurri and Spinach Salad

Time: 30 minutes
Preparation: 15 minutes
Cooking: 15 minutes
Servings: 4

INGREDIENTS

- For the Grilled Steak:
- 4 sirloin or ribeye steaks (about 1.5 pounds)
- 2 tablespoons olive oil
- 2 cloves garlic, minced
- 1 teaspoon dried oregano
- 1 teaspoon paprika
- Salt and black pepper to taste
- For the Chimichurri Sauce:
- 1 cup fresh parsley leaves, chopped
- 1/2 cup fresh cilantro leaves, chopped
- 4 cloves garlic, minced
- 1 o shallot, finely chopped
- 1/4 cup red wine vinegar
- 1/2 cup extra-virgin olive oil
- 1/2 teaspoon red pepper flakes (adjust to your spice preference)

- Salt and black pepper to taste
- For the Spinach Salad:
- 6 cups baby spinach
- 1/2 cup cherry tomatoes, halved
- 1/4 cup red onion, thinly sliced
- 1/4 cup feta cheese, crumbled
- 2 tablespoons balsamic vinaigrette dressing

INSTRUCTIONS

Grilled Steak:

1. Preheat Grill:
   - Preheat your grill to high heat.
2. Prepare Steak:
   - In a bowl, combine the olive oil, minced garlic, dried oregano, paprika, salt, and black pepper.
3. Rub Steak:
   - Rub the spice mixture all over the steaks.
4. Grill Steak:
   - Grill the steaks for about 4-5 minutes per side for medium-rare (adjust cooking time to your desired doneness).
   - Remove from the grill and let them rest for a few minutes.

Chimichurri Sauce:

1. Prepare Chimichurri:
   - In a bowl, combine the chopped parsley, chopped cilantro, minced garlic, chopped shallot, red wine vinegar, extra-virgin olive oil, red pepper flakes, salt, and black pepper.
   - Mix well to create the chimichurri sauce.

Spinach Salad:

1. Prepare Salad:
   - In a large bowl, combine the baby spinach, cherry tomatoes, thinly sliced red onion, and crumbled feta cheese.
2. Dress Salad:
   - Drizzle the balsamic vinaigrette dressing over the salad and toss to coat.

Serve:

   - Serve your Grilled Steak with a generous drizzle of chimichurri sauce and a side of spinach salad.

Nutritional Values (per serving, assuming 4 servings): Calories: 350 Kcal; Protein: 30g; Carbohydrates: 5g; Fat: 25g

Chicken Zoodle Soup

Time: 45 minutes
Preparation: 15 minutes
Cooking: 30 minutes
Servings: 4

INGREDIENTS

- For the Soup:
- 1 pound boneless, skinless chicken breasts
- 8 cups chicken broth
- 2 tablespoons olive oil
- 1 onion, chopped
- 2 carrots, sliced
- 2 celery stalks, sliced
- 2 cloves garlic, minced
- 1 teaspoon dried thyme
- 1 teaspoon dried rosemary
- Salt and black pepper to taste
- 2 cups zucchini noodles (zoodles)
- For Garnish:
- Fresh parsley, chopped

INSTRUCTIONS

Chicken Zoodle Soup:

1. Cook Chicken:
   - In a large pot, heat the olive oil over medium-high heat.
   - Add the chicken breasts and cook for about 6-8 minutes per side until they're no longer pink in the center.
   - Remove the chicken from the pot and set it aside to cool.
2. Sauté Veggies:
   - In the same pot, add the chopped onion, sliced carrots, and sliced celery.
   - Sauté for about 5 minutes until the vegetables start to soften.
3. Add Garlic and Spices:
   - Stir in the minced garlic, dried thyme, and dried rosemary. Cook for another 1-2 minutes until fragrant.
4. Simmer Soup:
   - Pour in the chicken broth and bring the soup to a simmer.
   - Let it simmer for about 15-20 minutes.

5. Shred Chicken:
   - While the soup simmers, shred the cooked chicken using two forks.
6. Add Chicken and Zoodles:
   - Add the shredded chicken and zucchini noodles to the soup.
   - Cook for an additional 5-7 minutes until the zoodles are tender.
7. Season:
   - Season the soup with salt and black pepper to taste.

Serve:
   - Serve your Chicken Zoodle Soup hot, garnished with chopped fresh parsley.

Nutritional Values (per serving, assuming 4 servings): Calories: 250 Kcal; Protein: 25g; Carbohydrates: 10g; Fat: 10g

Beef Stew with Root Vegetables

Time: 2.5 hours
Preparation: 15 minutes
Cooking: 2 hours and 15 minutes
Servings: 6

INGREDIENTS

- For the Beef Stew:
- 2 pounds beef stew meat, cut into 1-inch cubes
- 2 tablespoons olive oil
- 1 onion, chopped
- 2 cloves garlic, minced
- 4 cups beef broth
- 1 cup red wine (optional)
- 2 bay leaves
- 2 carrots, peeled and sliced
- 2 parsnips, peeled and sliced
- 2 turnips, peeled and diced
- 2 potatoes, peeled and diced
- 1 teaspoon dried thyme
- Salt and black pepper to taste
- For Garnish:
- Fresh parsley, chopped

INSTRUCTIONS

Beef Stew:
1. Brown Beef:
   - Heat the olive oil in a big pot with a heavy bottom over medium-high heat.
   - Add the beef cubes and brown them on all sides. Remove and set aside.
2. Sauté Onion and Garlic:
   - In the same pot, add the chopped onion and minced garlic.
   - Sauté for about 2-3 minutes until the onion becomes translucent.
3. Deglaze Pot:
   - If using red wine, pour it into the pot and use a spoon to scrape up any browned bits from the bottom.
4. Combine Ingredients:
   - Return the browned beef to the pot.
   - Add the beef broth, bay leaves, carrots, parsnips, turnips, potatoes, dried thyme, salt, and black pepper.
5. Simmer:
   - Bring the stew to a boil, then reduce the heat to low, cover, and simmer for about 2 hours or until the meat and vegetables are tender.
6. Remove Bay Leaves:
   - Before serving, don't forget to remove the bay leaves.

Serve:
   - Serve your Beef Stew with Root Vegetables, garnished with chopped fresh parsley.

Nutritional Values (per serving, assuming 6 servings): Calories: 350 Kcal; Protein: 30g; Carbohydrates: 15g; Fat: 15g

Lemon Herb Grilled Salmon with Asparagus

Time: 30 minutes
Preparation: 15 minutes
Cooking: 15 minutes
Servings: 4

INGREDIENTS

- For the Grilled Salmon:
- 4 salmon fillets (about 6 ounces each)
- 2 tablespoons olive oil

- 2 cloves garlic, minced
- 1 tablespoon fresh lemon juice
- 1 tablespoon fresh parsley, chopped
- 1 tablespoon fresh dill, chopped
- Salt and black pepper to taste
- 1 lemon, sliced for garnish
- For the Grilled Asparagus:
- 1 pound asparagus, trimmed
- 2 tablespoons olive oil
- Salt and black pepper to taste

INSTRUCTIONS

Grilled Salmon:

1. Preheat Grill:
   - Set your grill's temperature to medium-high.
2. Prepare Salmon:
   - In a bowl, combine the olive oil, minced garlic, lemon juice, chopped parsley, chopped dill, salt, and black pepper.
3. Marinate Salmon:
   - Brush the salmon fillets with the herb and lemon marinade.
4. Grill Salmon:
   - Place the salmon fillets on the preheated grill and cook for about 4-5 minutes per side until the salmon is opaque and flakes easily with a fork.

Grilled Asparagus:

1. Prepare Asparagus:
   - Toss the trimmed asparagus with olive oil, salt, and black pepper.
2. Grill Asparagus:
   - While grilling the salmon, you can also grill the asparagus. Place them directly on the grill grates for about 5-7 minutes until they are tender and slightly charred.

Serve:

- Serve your Lemon Herb Grilled Salmon with a side of grilled asparagus.
- Garnish with slices of lemon.

Nutritional Values (per serving, assuming 4 servings): Calories: 350 Kcal; Protein: 30g; Carbohydrates: 8g; Fat: 22g

Cilantro Lime Chicken with Avocado Salsa

Time: 30 minutes
Preparation: 15 minutes
Cooking: 15 minutes
Servings: 4

INGREDIENTS

- For the Cilantro Lime Chicken:
- 4 chicken breasts (about 6 ounces each)
- 2 tablespoons olive oil
- 2 cloves garlic, minced
- Zest and juice of 2 limes
- 1/4 cup fresh cilantro, chopped
- 1 teaspoon ground cumin
- Salt and black pepper to taste
- For the Avocado Salsa:
- 2 avocados, diced
- 1 cup cherry tomatoes, halved
- 1/2 red onion, finely chopped
- 1/4 cup fresh cilantro, chopped
- Juice of 1 lime
- Salt and black pepper to taste

INSTRUCTIONS

Cilantro Lime Chicken:

1. Prepare Chicken:
   - Season the chicken breasts with salt and black pepper.
2. Marinate Chicken:
   - In a bowl, combine the olive oil, minced garlic, lime zest, lime juice, chopped cilantro, and ground cumin.
   - Pour the marinade over the chicken breasts and allow them to marinate for at least 15 minutes.
3. Grill Chicken:
   - Set your grill's temperature to medium-high.
   - Grill the chicken for about 6-7 minutes per side, or until the chicken is no longer pink in the center and the internal temperature reaches 165°F (74°C).

Avocado Salsa:

1. Prepare Salsa:
   - In a separate bowl, combine the diced avocados, halved cherry tomatoes, finely

chopped red onion, chopped cilantro, lime juice, salt, and black pepper.
- Toss gently to combine.

Serve:
- Serve your Cilantro Lime Chicken hot, topped with the refreshing Avocado Salsa.

Nutritional Values (per serving, assuming 4 servings): Calories: 350 Kcal; Protein: 30g; Carbohydrates: 12g; Fat: 20g

Meatballs in Sugar-Free Marinara Sauce with Zucchini Spaghetti

Time: 1 hour
Preparation: 30 minutes
Cooking: 30 minutes
Servings: 4

INGREDIENTS
- For the Meatballs:
- 1 pound ground beef
- 1/2 pound ground pork
- 1/4 cup almond flour (as a binder)
- 1/4 cup Parmesan cheese, grated
- 1/4 cup fresh parsley, chopped
- 1 egg
- 2 cloves garlic, minced
- 1 teaspoon dried oregano
- Salt and black pepper to taste
- 2 tablespoons olive oil
- For the Sugar-Free Marinara Sauce:
- 1 can (28 oz) crushed tomatoes (check for no added sugar)
- 1 onion, finely chopped
- 2 cloves garlic, minced
- 1 teaspoon dried basil
- 1 teaspoon dried oregano
- 1/2 teaspoon red pepper flakes (adjust to your spice preference)
- Salt and black pepper to taste
- 2 tablespoons olive oil
- For the Zucchini Spaghetti:
- 4 zucchinis, spiralized into noodles
- 2 tablespoons olive oil
- Salt and black pepper to taste

INSTRUCTIONS

Meatballs:
1. Prepare Meatball Mixture:
   - In a bowl, combine the ground beef, ground pork, almond flour, grated Parmesan cheese, chopped parsley, egg, minced garlic, dried oregano, salt, and black pepper.
   - Mix well to combine all ingredients.
2. Shape Meatballs:
   - Form the mixture into meatballs, each about 1.5 inches in diameter.
3. Cook Meatballs:
   - Heat olive oil in a big skillet over medium heat.
   - Add the meatballs and cook for about 10-12 minutes, turning occasionally until they are browned and cooked through.
   - Remove the meatballs and set them aside.

Sugar-Free Marinara Sauce:
1. Sauté Onion and Garlic:
   - In the same skillet, add a bit more olive oil if needed.
   - Sauté the finely chopped onion and minced garlic for about 3-5 minutes until they become translucent.
2. Add Tomatoes and Spices:
   - Pour in the crushed tomatoes.
   - Add dried basil, dried oregano, red pepper flakes, salt, and black pepper.
   - Stir to combine.
3. Simmer Sauce:
   - Let the sauce simmer for about 15-20 minutes, allowing the flavors to meld.

Zucchini Spaghetti:
1. Prepare Zucchini Noodles:
   - Use a spiralizer to turn the zucchini into noodles.
2. Sauté Zucchini Noodles:
   - In a separate skillet, heat olive oil over medium heat.
   - Add the zucchini noodles and sauté for 2-3 minutes until they are tender but still crisp.
   - Season with salt and black pepper.

Serve:
- Serve your Meatballs in Sugar-Free Marinara Sauce over a bed of zucchini spaghetti.
- You can optionally add fresh parsley and grated Parmesan cheese as garnish.

Nutritional Values (per serving, assuming 4 servings): Calories: 450 Kcal; Protein: 30g; Carbohydrates: 10g; Fat: 30g

Coconut Chicken Alfredo

Time: 30 minutes Preparation: 15 minutes
Cooking: 15 minutes Servings: 4

INGREDIENTS

- For the Coconut Chicken:
- 2 chicken breasts (about 8 ounces each)
- 2 tablespoons olive oil
- 1 can (14 oz) coconut milk
- 2 cloves garlic, minced
- 1 teaspoon dried basil
- Salt and black pepper to taste
- 2 tablespoons fresh cilantro, chopped (for garnish)
- For the Alfredo Sauce:
- 2 cups heavy cream
- 1/2 cup Parmesan cheese, grated
- 2 tablespoons butter
- 2 cloves garlic, minced
- 1 teaspoon dried parsley
- Salt and black pepper to taste
- For Serving:
- 12 ounces fettuccine pasta
- Grated Parmesan cheese (for garnish)

INSTRUCTIONS

Coconut Chicken:
1. Prepare Chicken:
   - Season the chicken breasts with salt and black pepper.
2. Cook Chicken:
   - Heat olive oil in a big skillet over medium heat.
   - Once the chicken breasts are no longer pink in the middle, add them and cook for about 6-7 minutes on each side.
   - Remove the chicken and set it aside.
3. Prepare Coconut Sauce:
   - In the same skillet, add minced garlic, dried basil, and the entire can of coconut milk.
   - After stirring, boil for three to four minutes, or until the sauce slightly thickens.

Alfredo Sauce:
1. Prepare Alfredo Sauce:
   - In another skillet, melt the butter over medium heat.
   - Once aromatic, add the minced garlic and sauté it for one to two minutes.
   - Add the dried parsley, grated Parmesan cheese, black pepper, and heavy cream.
   - Stir until the cheese is completely melted and the sauce thickens.

Pasta:
1. Cook Fettuccine:
   - Cook the fettuccine pasta according to the package instructions until al dente.
   - Drain and set aside.

Serve:
   - Slice the cooked chicken into strips.
   - Serve the coconut chicken over a bed of fettuccine pasta, drizzled with the creamy Alfredo sauce.
   - Add grated Parmesan cheese and fresh cilantro as garnishes.

Nutritional Values (per serving, assuming 4 servings): Calories: 750 Kcal; Protein: 30g; Carbohydrates: 50g; Fat: 50g

Spinach and Ricotta Stuffed Chicken Thighs

Time: 1 hour
Preparation: 20 minutes
Cooking: 40 minutes
Servings: 4

INGREDIENTS

- For the Stuffed Chicken Thighs:
- 4 boneless, skinless chicken thighs
- 1 cup fresh spinach, chopped
- 1 cup ricotta cheese
- 1/2 cup mozzarella cheese, shredded
- 1/4 cup Parmesan cheese, grated
- 2 cloves garlic, minced
- 1 egg
- 1 teaspoon dried basil
- 1 teaspoon dried oregano
- Salt and black pepper to taste
- Toothpicks or kitchen twine
- For the Sauce:

- 1 can (14 oz) crushed tomatoes
- 1/2 teaspoon dried basil
- 1/2 teaspoon dried oregano
- Salt and black pepper to taste
- For Garnish:
- Fresh basil leaves, chopped
- Grated Parmesan cheese

INSTRUCTIONS

Stuffed Chicken Thighs:

1. Prepare Chicken Thighs:
   - Season the chicken thighs with salt and black pepper.
2. Prepare Stuffing Mixture:
   - In a bowl, combine the chopped spinach, ricotta cheese, mozzarella cheese, Parmesan cheese, minced garlic, egg, dried basil, dried oregano, salt, and black pepper.
3. Stuff Chicken Thighs:
   - Carefully create a pocket in each chicken thigh by making a small incision along the side.
   - Stuff the spinach and ricotta mixture into each thigh.
   - Use kitchen twine or toothpicks to seal the openings.
4. Sear and Bake:
   - Heat a small amount of olive oil in an ovenproof skillet over medium-high heat.
   - Sear the stuffed chicken thighs for about 2-3 minutes per side until they are browned.
   - Remove from heat.

Sauce:

1. Prepare Sauce:
   - Combine the crushed tomatoes, salt, black pepper, dried oregano, and dried basil in a small bowl.
2. Spoon Sauce Over Chicken:
   - Pour the sauce over the seared chicken thighs.
3. Bake:
   - Place the skillet in a preheated oven at 375°F (190°C) and bake for about 30 minutes or until the chicken is cooked through.

Serve:

- Serve your Spinach and Ricotta Stuffed Chicken Thighs hot, garnished with chopped fresh basil and grated Parmesan cheese.

Nutritional Values (per serving, assuming 4 servings): Calories: 350 Kcal; Protein: 30g; Carbohydrates: 10g; Fat: 20g

Pesto Zucchini Noodles with Grilled Prawns

Time: 30 minutes
Preparation: 15 minutes
Cooking: 15 minutes
Servings: 4

INGREDIENTS

- For the Pesto:
- 2 cups fresh basil leaves
- 1/2 cup Parmesan cheese, grated
- 1/2 cup pine nuts
- 2 cloves garlic, minced
- 1/2 cup extra-virgin olive oil
- Juice of 1 lemon
- Salt and black pepper to taste
- For the Zucchini Noodles:
- 4 large zucchinis, spiralized into noodles
- 2 tablespoons olive oil
- Salt and black pepper to taste
- For the Grilled Prawns:
- 1 pound prawns (shrimp), peeled and deveined
- 2 tablespoons olive oil
- 1 teaspoon dried oregano
- Salt and black pepper to taste
- Lemon wedges for garnish

INSTRUCTIONS

Pesto:

1. Prepare Pesto:
   - In a food processor, combine the fresh basil leaves, grated Parmesan cheese, pine nuts, minced garlic, lemon juice, salt, and black pepper.
   - While the food processor is running, slowly drizzle in the extra-virgin olive oil until the pesto is smooth and well-blended.

Zucchini Noodles:

1. Prepare Zucchini Noodles:
   - Use a spiralizer to turn the zucchini into noodles.

2. Sauté Zucchini Noodles:
   - Heat olive oil in a big skillet over medium heat.
   - Add the zucchini noodles and sauté for about 2-3 minutes until they are tender but still crisp.
   - Season with salt and black pepper.

Grilled Prawns:

1. Prepare Prawns:
   - In a bowl, combine the prawns, olive oil, dried oregano, salt, and black pepper.
   - Toss to coat.
2. Grill Prawns:
   - Set your grill's temperature to medium-high.
   - Thread the prawns onto skewers.
   - Cook on the grill for 2 to 3 minutes on each side, or until they are cooked through and pink.

Serve:
   - Serve your Pesto Zucchini Noodles with Grilled Prawns.
   - Drizzle the pesto over the zucchini noodles, top with the grilled prawns, and garnish with lemon wedges.

Nutritional Values (per serving, assuming 4 servings): Calories: 350 Kcal; Protein: 20g; Carbohydrates: 10g; Fat: 25g

Rosemary Lamb Stew with Turnips

Time: 2.5 hours
Preparation: 20 minutes
Cooking: 2 hours and 10 minutes
Servings: 6

INGREDIENTS

- For the Stew:
- 2 pounds of lamb stew meat, cubed
- 2 tablespoons olive oil
- 2 onions, chopped
- 3 cloves garlic, minced
- 4 cups beef broth
- 2 turnips, peeled and diced
- 3 carrots, peeled and sliced
- 2 ocelery stalks, sliced
- 1 tablespoon fresh rosemary, chopped
- 1 bay leaf
- Salt and black pepper to taste
- For Garnish:
- Fresh parsley, chopped

INSTRUCTIONS

Stew:
1. Prepare Lamb:
   - Season the lamb stew meat with salt and black pepper.
2. Sear Lamb:
   - In a large, heavy-bottomed pot, heat the olive oil over medium-high heat.
   - Add the lamb and brown it on all sides.
   - Remove the lamb and set it aside.
3. Sauté Onions and Garlic:
   - In the same pot, add the chopped onions and minced garlic.
   - Sauté the onions for three to five minutes, or until they are transparent.
4. Deglaze Pot:
   - Pour in a bit of the beef broth to deglaze the pot, scraping up any browned bits from the bottom.
5. Combine Ingredients:
   - Place the browned lamb back in the pot.
   - Add the remaining beef broth, diced turnips, sliced carrots, sliced celery, chopped rosemary, bay leaf, salt, and black pepper.
6. Simmer Stew:
   - After bringing the stew to a boil, lower the heat to a simmer, cover it, and let it cook for one to two hours, or until the lamb is fork-tender and the veggies are thoroughly cooked.

Serve:
   - Top your warm rosemary lamb stew with chopped fresh parsley and turnips.

Nutritional Values (per serving, assuming 6 servings): Calories: 350 Kcal; Protein: 30g; Carbohydrates: 15g; Fat: 15g

Spaghetti Squash Carbonara with Bacon

Time: 1 hour
Preparation: 20 minutes
Cooking: 40 minutes
Servings: 4

INGREDIENTS

- For the Spaghetti Squash:
- 2 medium spaghetti squash
- 2 tablespoons olive oil
- Salt and black pepper to taste
- For the Carbonara Sauce:
- 6 slices bacon, chopped
- 1 onion, finely chopped
- 2 cloves garlic, minced
- 3 egg yolks
- 1/2 cup heavy cream
- 1 cup Parmesan cheese, grated
- Salt and black pepper to taste
- Fresh parsley, chopped (for garnish)

INSTRUCTIONS

Spaghetti Squash:
1. Prepare Squash:
   - Preheat your oven to 375°F (190°C).
   - Remove the seeds after cutting the spaghetti squash in half lengthwise.
   - Brush the inside with olive oil and season with salt and black pepper.
2. Roast Squash:
   - Arrange the squash halves on a baking pan, cut side down.
   - Roast them in the preheated oven for about 30-40 minutes or until the flesh is tender and easily scrapes into strands with a fork.
   - After letting it cool down a little, use a fork to scrape the squash into strands.

Carbonara Sauce:
1. Sauté Bacon and Onion:
   - In a large skillet, cook the chopped bacon over medium heat until it's crispy.
   - Remove some of the excess bacon fat, leaving about 1-2 tablespoons in the skillet.
   - Add the minced garlic and chopped onion, and sauté for three to five minutes, or until the onion is transparent.
2. Prepare Carbonara Mixture:
   - Combine the heavy cream, grated Parmesan cheese, and egg yolks in a bowl.
3. Combine Ingredients:
   - Combine the cooked and drained spaghetti squash with the onion and bacon in the skillet.
   - Pour the carbonara mixture over the squash, stirring quickly to combine.
4. Season and Serve:
   - To taste, add salt and black pepper for seasoning.
   - Cook for an additional 2-3 minutes, stirring gently until the sauce thickens.
   - Serve your Spaghetti Squash Carbonara hot, garnished with chopped fresh parsley.

Nutritional Values (per serving, assuming 4 servings): Calories: 350 Kcal; Protein: 15g; Carbohydrates: 15g; Fat: 25g

Avocado and Tuna Salad Cups

Time: 20 minutes
Preparation: 20 minutes
Servings: 4

INGREDIENTS

- For the Tuna Salad:
- 2 cans (5 oz each) of tuna in water, drained
- 1/4 cup mayonnaise
- 1/4 cup Greek yogurt
- 2 tablespoons fresh lemon juice
- 2 tablespoons fresh dill, chopped
- 1 celery stalk, finely chopped
- 1/4 cup red onion, finely chopped
- Salt and black pepper to taste
- For the Avocado Cups:
- 2 avocados, halved and pitted
- 1 lemon, cut into wedges (for garnish)
- Lettuce leaves (for serving)

INSTRUCTIONS

Tuna Salad:
1. Prepare Tuna Salad:
   - In a bowl, combine the drained tuna, mayonnaise, Greek yogurt, fresh lemon juice, chopped dill, chopped celery, and chopped red onion.
   - Mix well to combine all the ingredients.
   - To taste, add salt and black pepper for seasoning.

Avocado Cups:
1. Prepare Avocado Halves:
   - Halve and pit the avocados.
   - Squeeze some lemon juice over the avocado halves to prevent browning.
2. Create Hollows:
   - To make hollow cups, carefully scrape out a small portion of flesh from each avocado half.

Serve:
1. Fill Avocado Cups:
   - Place a lettuce leaf in each serving dish.
   - Fill each avocado cup with the prepared tuna salad.

2. Garnish and Serve:
   - Garnish the Avocado and Tuna Salad Cups with fresh dill and lemon wedges.
   - Serve immediately.

Nutritional Values (per serving, assuming 4 servings): Calories: 250 Kcal; Protein: 15g; Carbohydrates: 8g; Fat: 18g

Spinach and Feta Stuffed Mushrooms

Time: 30 minutes
Preparation: 15 minutes
Cooking: 15 minutes
Servings: 4

INGREDIENTS

- 16 large mushrooms, cleaned and stems removed
- 2 cups spinach, chopped
- 1/2 cup feta cheese, crumbled
- 2 cloves garlic, minced
- 1/4 cup onion, finely chopped
- 2 tablespoons olive oil
- 1/4 cup breadcrumbs
- 2 tablespoons fresh parsley, chopped
- Salt and black pepper to taste

INSTRUCTIONS

1. Prepare Mushrooms:
   - Preheat your oven to 375°F (190°C).
   - Clean the mushrooms and remove the stems.
   - Place the mushroom caps on a baking sheet.
2. Sauté Spinach, Garlic, and Onion:
   - In a skillet, heat the olive oil over medium heat.
   - Add the minced garlic and diced onion, and sauté for two to three minutes, or until they are transparent.
   - Add the chopped spinach and cook for an additional 2-3 minutes until the spinach wilts.
   - Remove from heat.
3. Prepare Stuffing:
   - In a bowl, combine the sautéed spinach mixture, crumbled feta cheese, breadcrumbs, and chopped parsley.
   - To taste, add salt and black pepper for seasoning.

4. Stuff Mushrooms:
   - Spoon the spinach and feta mixture into each mushroom cap.
5. Bake:
   - Bake the stuffed mushrooms for 12 to 15 minutes, or until the filling is golden brown and the mushrooms are soft.
6. Serve:
   - Garnish your hot spinach and feta stuffed mushrooms with more chopped parsley, if you'd like.

Nutritional Values (per serving, assuming 4 servings): Calories: 150 Kcal; Protein: 7g; Carbohydrates: 10g; Fat: 10g

Baked Kale Chips with Sea Salt

Time: 25 minutes
Preparation: 10 minutes
Cooking: 15 minutes
Servings: 4

INGREDIENTS

- 1 bunch of kale
- 1 tablespoon olive oil
- Sea salt, to taste

INSTRUCTIONS

1. Preheat Oven:
   - Set the oven temperature to 175°C, or 350°F.
2. Prepare Kale:
   - Wash and thoroughly dry the kale leaves.
   - Break the leaves off into bite-sized pieces and remove the tough stems.
3. Toss with Olive Oil:
   - In a large bowl, toss the kale pieces with olive oil, ensuring they are evenly coated.
4. Arrange on Baking Sheet:
   - Spread the kale pieces in a single layer on a baking sheet. If necessary, use multiple baking sheets to prevent crowding.
5. Bake:
   - Bake the kale for ten to fifteen minutes in a preheated oven, or until crisp but not browned. They may go from crisp to burnt very rapidly, so watch them carefully.

6. Season with Sea Salt:
   - While the kale chips are still warm, sprinkle them with sea salt to taste.
7. Cool and Serve:
   - Allow the kale chips to cool before serving. When they cool, they will keep getting crispier.

Nutritional Values (per serving, assuming 4 servings): Calories: 50 Kcal; Protein: 2g; Carbohydrates: 5g; Fat: 3g

Macadamia Nut Clusters with Dark Chocolate

Time: 15 minutes
Preparation: 10 minutes
Chilling: 30 minutes
Servings: Varies

INGREDIENTS

- 1 cup macadamia nuts
- 8 ounces dark chocolate, chopped
- 1 tablespoon coconut oil
- 1/4 cup unsweetened shredded coconut
- Sea salt for sprinkling (optional)

INSTRUCTIONS

1. Prepare a Baking Sheet:
   - Line a baking sheet with parchment paper or a silicone baking mat.
2. Melt Chocolate:
   - In a microwave-safe bowl or using a double boiler, melt the dark chocolate and oil together until smooth. Stir regularly to prevent burning.
3. Combine Nuts and Coconut:
   - In a separate bowl, combine the macadamia nuts and shredded coconut.
4. Create Clusters:
   - Spoon small portions of the melted chocolate onto the prepared baking sheet to create clusters.
5. Add Nut Mixture:
   - While the chocolate is still soft, press the macadamia nut and coconut mixture into the chocolate clusters. They are customizable to your desired size.
6. Chill:
   - Sprinkle a pinch of sea salt on each cluster if desired.
   - Chill the baking sheet in the fridge for approximately half an hour, or until the chocolate is set.
7. Serve:
   - Once the clusters have been set, remove them from the refrigerator.
   - Carefully peel them from the parchment paper or silicone baking mat.
   - Serve and enjoy your Macadamia Nut Clusters with Dark Chocolate.

Note: To keep them fresh, you can keep any excess clusters in the refrigerator in an airtight container.

Nutritional Values: Depending on how big and how many clusters you construct, as well as the brands of components you use, the nutritional values will change.

Coconut Milk Berry Popsicles

Time: 10 minutes (plus freezing time)
Preparation: 10 minutes
Freezing: 4 hours or until firm
Servings: 6 popsicles

INGREDIENTS

- 1 cup mixed berries (strawberries, blueberries, raspberries)
- 1 can (13.5 oz) coconut milk
- 1/4 cup honey or maple syrup (adjust to taste)
- 1 teaspoon vanilla extract

INSTRUCTIONS

1. Prepare Berries:
   - Wash and chop the mixed berries, if needed.
2. Blend Ingredients:
   - In a blender, combine the coconut milk, honey or maple syrup, and vanilla extract. Blend the mixture until it's well incorporated and smooth.
3. Layer the Popsicles:
   - In your popsicle molds, alternate layers of the blended coconut milk mixture and the

chopped berries. You can use a popsicle stick to gently swirl the layers together for a marbled effect.

4. Insert Sticks:
   * Insert popsicle sticks into each mold.
5. Freeze:
   * After putting the popsicle moulds in the freezer, leave them there for at least four hours, or until they solidify fully.
6. Unmold and Serve:
   * When ready to eat, pour some warm water over the exterior of the moulds for a few seconds to loosen the popsicles and then remove them from the moulds. Gently pull the popsicles out.
   * Serve your Coconut Milk Berry Popsicles immediately and savor the refreshing flavors.

Nutritional Values (per popsicle, assuming 6 servings): Calories: 120 Kcal; Protein: 1g; Carbohydrates: 12g; Fat: 8g

Cucumber and Salmon Bite-sized Sandwiches

Time: 15 minutes
Preparation: 15 minutes
Servings: Varies

INGREDIENTS

* 1 cucumber
* 4 oz smoked wild-caught salmon
* 4 oz cream cheese
* 2 tablespoons fresh dill, chopped
* 1 tablespoon lemon juice
* Salt and black pepper to taste

INSTRUCTIONS

1. Prepare Cucumber:
   * Wash and peel the cucumber. Cut it into thin slices.
2. Prepare Salmon Filling:
   * In a bowl, combine the cream cheese, chopped dill, and lemon juice. Mix until well combined.
   * To taste, add a dash of salt and black pepper for seasoning.

3. Assemble Sandwiches:
   * Apply a thin layer of the cream cheese mixture on a slice of cucumber.
   * Place a smoked salmon slice on top of the combination of cream cheese.
   * Place another slice of cucumber on top to make a "sandwich."
4. Garnish:
   * Garnish the sandwiches with a small sprig of fresh dill.
5. Serve:
   * Arrange your Cucumber and Salmon Bite-sized Sandwiches on a serving platter.

Nutritional Values: The quantity of sandwiches you create and the particular brands of products you choose will affect the nutritional values.

Chia Seed and Coconut Milk Pudding

Time: 5 minutes (plus chilling time)
Preparation: 5 minutes
Chilling: 2-4 hours or overnight
Servings: 4

INGREDIENTS

* 1 can (13.5 oz) full-fat coconut milk
* 1/2 cup chia seeds
* 2-3 tablespoons honey or maple syrup (adjust to taste)
* 1 teaspoon vanilla extract
* Fresh berries for garnish (e.g., strawberries, blueberries, raspberries)

INSTRUCTIONS

1. Mix Ingredients:
   * In a mixing bowl, combine the full-fat coconut milk, chia seeds, honey or maple syrup, and vanilla extract.
   * Give it a good stir to make sure the chia seeds are dispersed equally.
2. Chill:
   * Place a lid on the bowl and chill the mixture for a minimum of two to four hours or overnight. This enables the liquid to seep into the chia seeds, giving them a pudding-like consistency.

3. Stir:
   * Make sure the custard is well combined by giving it a thorough stir after the chilling time.
4. Serve:
   * Portion the Chia Seed and Coconut Milk Pudding into serving dishes.
   * Top with fresh berries or other fruit of your choice.

Nutritional Values (per serving, assuming 4 servings): Calories: 300 Kcal; Protein: 6g; Carbohydrates: 20g; Fat: 23g

Zucchini and Parmesan Crisps

Time: 30 minutes
Preparation: 15 minutes
Cooking: 15 minutes
Servings: 4

INGREDIENTS

* 2 medium zucchinis
* 1/2 cup Parmesan cheese, grated
* 1/4 cup breadcrumbs (gluten-free, if desired)
* 1/2 teaspoon garlic powder
* 1/2 teaspoon onion powder
* 1/2 teaspoon dried oregano
* 1/4 teaspoon paprika
* Salt and black pepper, to taste
* 2 eggs, beaten
* Cooking spray or olive oil for greasing

INSTRUCTIONS

1. Preheat Oven:
   * Preheat your oven to 425°F (220°C).
2. Prepare Zucchinis:
   * Wash the zucchini and slice them into thin rounds.
3. Prepare Coating:
   * In a bowl, combine the grated Parmesan cheese, breadcrumbs, garlic powder, onion powder, dried oregano, paprika, salt, and black pepper. Mix well.
4. Coat Zucchini Slices:
   * Dip each zucchini slice into the beaten eggs, allowing any excess to drip off.
   * Next, lightly press the zucchini slice to

adhere to the coating after covering it with the Parmesan breadcrumb mixture.
5. Arrange on Baking Sheet:
   * Place the coated zucchini slices on a baking sheet that's been lightly greased with cooking spray or olive oil.
6. Bake:
   * Bake the crispy and golden-brown zucchini chips for 12 to 15 minutes in a preheated oven..
7. Serve:
   * Serve your Zucchini and Parmesan Crisps hot as a snack or appetizer.

Nutritional Values (per serving, assuming 4 servings): Calories: 160 Kcal; Protein: 10g; Carbohydrates: 10g; Fat: 9g

Egg and Spinach Muffins

Time: 30 minutes
Preparation: 15 minutes
Cooking: 15 minutes
Servings: 6 muffins

INGREDIENTS

* 6 eggs
* 1 cup spinach, chopped
* 1/4 cup bell pepper, finely diced
* 1/4 cup red onion, finely diced
* 1/4 cup cheddar cheese, grated
* 1/4 cup milk (dairy or dairy-free)
* 1/2 teaspoon garlic powder
* 1/2 teaspoon dried oregano
* Salt and black pepper, to taste
* Cooking spray or olive oil for greasing

INSTRUCTIONS

1. Preheat Oven:
   * Set the oven temperature to 175°C, or 350°F.
2. Prepare Muffin Tin:
   * Use cooking spray or a tiny bit of olive oil to lightly grease a muffin pan.
3. Whisk Eggs:
   * In a bowl, whisk the eggs and milk together until well combined.
4. Add Vegetables:
   * Stir in the chopped spinach, finely diced bell pepper, finely diced red onion, grated

cheddar cheese, garlic powder, dried oregano, salt, and black pepper to the egg mixture. Mix well.

5. Pour into Muffin Tin:
   - Pour the egg and vegetable mixture evenly into the prepared muffin tin.
6. Bake:
   - Bake for 12 to 15 minutes, or until the muffins are set and the tops are beginning to turn brown, in a preheated oven..
7. Serve:
   - Allow the Egg and Spinach Muffins to cool for a few minutes before removing them from the muffin tin. They can be served room temperature or warm.

Nutritional Values (per muffin, assuming 6 muffins): Calories: 100 Kcal; Protein: 7g; Carbohydrates: 3g; Fat: 6g

Walnut and Dark Chocolate Energy Balls

Time: 15 minutes (plus chilling time)
Preparation: 15 minutes
Chilling: 30 minutes
Servings: 12-16 balls

INGREDIENTS

- 1 cup walnuts
- 1/2 cup rolled oats
- 1/4 cup dark chocolate chips
- 1/4 cup honey or maple syrup
- 1/4 cup almond butter
- 1 tablespoon chia seeds
- 1/2 teaspoon vanilla extract
- A pinch of sea salt

INSTRUCTIONS

1. Prepare Ingredients:
   - In a food processor, pulse the walnuts and rolled oats until they are finely chopped but not too fine. Transfer to a bowl.
2. Mix Dry Ingredients:
   - To the bowl with the chopped walnuts and oats, add the dark chocolate chips and chia seeds. Mix to combine.
3. Prepare Wet Ingredients:
   - In a separate bowl, combine the honey or

maple syrup, almond butter, vanilla extract, and a pinch of sea salt. Stir until well mixed.

4. Combine Ingredients:
   - After adding the wet components to the dry ingredients, whisk everything together until thoroughly mixed.
5. Shape into Balls:
   - Using your hands, roll little parts of the mixture into compact balls. You can dampen your hands a little bit to avoid sticking if the mixture is excessively sticky.
6. Chill:
   - Place the Walnut and Dark Chocolate Energy Balls on a baking sheet or plate and refrigerate for about 30 minutes or until they firm up.
7. Serve:
   - Once they are chilled, your energy balls are ready to enjoy. Any extras should be kept in the refrigerator in an airtight container.

Nutritional Values (per ball, assuming 14 balls): Calories: 120 Kcal; Protein: 3g; Carbohydrates: 9g; Fat: 8g

Baked Asparagus Fries with Garlic Aioli

Time: 30 minutes
Preparation: 15 minutes
Cooking: 15 minutes
Servings: 4

INGREDIENTS

- For the Baked Asparagus Fries:
- 1 bunch of asparagus
- 1/2 cup whole wheat or almond flour
- 2 eggs, beaten
- 1 cup panko breadcrumbs
- 1/4 cup Parmesan cheese, grated
- 1/2 teaspoon garlic powder
- 1/2 teaspoon dried oregano
- Salt and black pepper, to taste
- Cooking spray or olive oil for greasing
- For the Garlic Aioli:
- 1/2 cup mayonnaise
- 1 clove garlic, minced
- 1 tablespoon lemon juice
- 1/2 teaspoon dried dill

- Salt and black pepper, to taste

INSTRUCTIONS

For the Baked Asparagus Fries:

1. Preheat Oven:
   - Preheat your oven to 425°F (220°C).
2. Prepare Asparagus:
   - Wash the asparagus and trim the tough ends.
3. Coat Asparagus:
   - In one bowl, place the whole wheat or almond flour.
   - In a second bowl, place the beaten eggs.
   - In a third bowl, combine the panko breadcrumbs, grated Parmesan cheese, garlic powder, dried oregano, salt, and black pepper.
4. Dip and Coat:
   - Take an asparagus spear, dip it in the flour, then the beaten egg, and finally, coat it with the breadcrumb mixture. Make sure the coating is thick.
   - Spread some cooking spray or olive oil on a baking pan and arrange the coated asparagus on it.
5. Bake:
   - Bake for 12 to 15 minutes in a preheated oven, or until the asparagus is soft and the coating is crispy and golden.

For the Garlic Aioli:

1. Prepare Aioli:
   - Combine the mayonnaise, dried dill, lemon juice, minced garlic, salt, and black pepper in a small bowl. Stir until well mixed.
2. Serve:
   - Serve your Baked Asparagus Fries with the Garlic Aioli as a dipping sauce.

Nutritional Values (per serving, assuming 4 servings): Calories: 200 Kcal (asparagus fries, excluding aioli); Protein: 8g; Carbohydrates: 20g; Fat: 9g

Coconut Butter and Berry Fat Bombs

Time: 15 minutes (plus chilling time)
Preparation: 15 minutes
Chilling: 1-2 hours
Servings: 12 fat bombs

INGREDIENTS

- 1/2 cup coconut butter
- 1/4 cup coconut oil
- 1/4 cup mixed berries (e.g., strawberries, blueberries, raspberries), chopped
- 2 tablespoons honey or maple syrup (adjust to taste)
- 1/2 teaspoon vanilla extract
- A pinch of sea salt

INSTRUCTIONS

1. Prepare Ingredients:
   - In a microwave-safe bowl or using a double boiler, melt the coconut butter and coconut oil until they are fully liquid.
2. Add Sweetener and Flavor:
   - Stir in the honey or maple syrup, vanilla extract, and a pinch of sea salt. Mix until well combined.
3. Add Berries:
   - Gently fold in the chopped mixed berries.
4. Fill Molds:
   - Pour the mixture into silicone molds or ice cube trays. Additionally, you can use little silicone muffin cups.
5. Chill:
   - Refrigerate the trays or moulds for one to two hours, or until the fat bombs set..
6. Serve:
   - Once they are set, remove the fat bombs from the molds or trays.

Nutritional Values (per fat bomb, assuming 12 fat bombs): Calories: 100 Kcal; Protein: 1g; Carbohydrates: 3g; Fat: 10g

Almond and Herb Stuffed Olives

Time: 15 minutes
Preparation: 15 minutes
Servings: Varies

INGREDIENTS

- 1 cup green olives, pitted
- 1/4 cup almonds
- 1 clove garlic, minced
- 2 tablespoons fresh parsley, finely chopped
- 2 tablespoons lemon zest
- 1 tablespoon olive oil
- A pinch of red pepper flakes (optional)

INSTRUCTIONS

1. Prepare Olives:
   - Rinse the green olives and allow them to drain.
2. Make Almond Filling:
   - In a food processor, combine the almonds, minced garlic, chopped fresh parsley, lemon zest, olive oil, and red pepper flakes if you desire a little heat. Process until a coarse paste forms from the ingredients.
3. Stuff Olives:
   - Gently open each olive by making a small cut lengthwise.
   - Stuff each olive with the almond and herb mixture. For this, you can use your fingers or a little spoon.
4. Serve:
   - Serve your Almond and Herb Stuffed Olives as a delicious appetiser by arranging them on a serving dish.

Nutritional Values: The quantity of olives you stuff and the particular brands of ingredients you use will affect the nutritional values.

Cheese and Walnut Stuffed Bell Peppers

Time: 45 minutes
Preparation: 15 minutes
Cooking: 30 minutes
Servings: 4

INGREDIENTS

- 4 bell peppers (red, yellow, or green)
- 1 cup ricotta cheese
- 1/2 cup walnuts, chopped
- 1/4 cup Parmesan cheese, grated
- 2 tablespoons fresh basil, chopped
- 1 clove garlic, minced
- Salt and black pepper, to taste
- Olive oil for drizzling

INSTRUCTIONS

1. Preheat Oven:
   - Set the oven temperature to 175°C, or 350°F.
2. Prepare Bell Peppers:
   - Remove the seeds and membranes from the bell peppers by cutting off the tops. After rinsing them, put them aside.
3. Make Filling:
   - In a bowl, combine the ricotta cheese, chopped walnuts, grated Parmesan cheese, chopped fresh basil, minced garlic, salt, and black pepper. Mix until the filling is well combined.
4. Stuff Peppers:
   - Carefully stuff each bell pepper with the cheese and walnut mixture.
5. Arrange in Baking Dish:
   - The stuffed bell peppers should be put in a baking dish.
6. Drizzle with Olive Oil:
   - Drizzle the tops of the stuffed peppers with a bit of olive oil.
7. Bake:
   - Bake the baking dish in the preheated oven for about thirty minutes, or until the peppers are soft, covered with foil.
8. Serve:
   - Remove from the oven and serve your Cheese and Walnut Stuffed Bell Peppers as a delicious and savory dish.

Nutritional Values (per serving, assuming 4 servings): Calories: 250 Kcal; Protein: 10g; Carbohydrates: 10g; Fat: 19g

Spicy Guacamole with Celery Sticks

Time: 15 minutes
Preparation: 15 minutes
Servings: 4

INGREDIENTS

- For the Spicy Guacamole:
- 3 ripe avocados, peeled and pitted
- jalapeño pepper, seeded and minced (adjust to your preferred level of spiciness)
- 1/4 cup red onion, finely chopped
- 1/4 cup fresh cilantro, chopped
- 2 tablespoons lime juice
- 1 clove garlic, minced
- Salt and black pepper, to taste
- For the Celery Sticks:
- 4 celery stalks, washed and cut into sticks

INSTRUCTIONS

For the Spicy Guacamole:
1. Prepare Avocado:
   - In a bowl, mash the ripe avocados using a fork until you achieve your preferred level of smoothness.
2. Add Ingredients:
   - Add the minced jalapeño pepper, finely chopped red onion, fresh cilantro, lime juice, minced garlic, salt, and black pepper to the mashed avocado. Mix well.
3. Adjust Seasoning:
   - Taste the guacamole and adjust the level of spiciness, salt, or lime juice as needed.
4. Serve:
   - Serve your Spicy Guacamole with the celery sticks.

Nutritional Values (per serving, assuming 4 servings): Calories: 200 Kcal (guacamole, excluding celery sticks); Protein: 3g; Carbohydrates: 14g; Fat: 16g

Pork Rind Nachos

Time: 15 minutes
Preparation: 15 minutes
Servings: 4

INGREDIENTS

- 2 cups pork rinds
- 1 cup cheddar cheese, shredded
- 1/2 cup sour cream
- 1/4 cup salsa
- 1/4 cup green onions, chopped
- 1/4 cup black olives, sliced
- 1/4 cup jalapeño peppers, sliced (adjust to your preferred level of spiciness)
- 1/4 cup guacamole (optional)
- 1/4 cup fresh cilantro, chopped (for garnish)
- Salt and black pepper, to taste

INSTRUCTIONS

1. Prepare Pork Rind Base:
   - Arrange the pork rinds on a large serving platter or individual plates.
2. Add Cheese:
   - Sprinkle the cheddar cheese evenly over the pork rinds.
3. Melt:
   - Place the pork rinds and cheese in the microwave or under the broiler until the cheese is melted and bubbly.
4. Add Toppings:
   - While the cheese is still hot, add the sour cream, salsa, chopped green onions, sliced black olives, and sliced jalapeño peppers.
5. Garnish:
   - If desired, garnish with dollops of guacamole and a sprinkle of chopped fresh cilantro.
6. Season:
   - Season your Pork Rind Nachos with a pinch of salt and black pepper to taste.
7. Serve:
   - Serve immediately, and enjoy your low-carb and crunchy nacho delight!

Nutritional Values (per serving, assuming 4 servings): Calories: 300 Kcal; Protein: 12g; Carbohydrates: 4g; Fat: 27g

Flaxseed and Parmesan Crackers

Time: 35 minutes
Preparation: 15 minutes
Baking: 20 minutes
Servings: Varies (depends on the size of your crackers)

INGREDIENTS

- 1 cup ground flaxseed
- 1/2 cup grated Parmesan cheese
- 1 teaspoon garlic powder
- 1 teaspoon dried oregano
- 1/2 teaspoon onion powder
- 1/4 teaspoon sea salt
- 1/4 teaspoon black pepper
- 1/2 cup water
- Olive oil for greasing

INSTRUCTIONS

1. Preheat Oven:
   - Set the oven temperature to 175°C, or 350°F.
2. Mix Dry Ingredients:
   - In a bowl, combine the ground flaxseed, grated Parmesan cheese, garlic powder, dried oregano, onion powder, sea salt, and black pepper. Mix well to combine the dry ingredients.
3. Add Water:
   - Add the water to the dry ingredients and stir until you have a thick, cohesive mixture. To enable the flaxseed to absorb some of the water, let it sit for a few minutes.
4. Roll Out Dough:
   - Place the dough between two sheets of parchment paper. Roll it out to the desired thickness with a rolling pin. The crackers will be crispier the thinner you roll it.
5. Cut into Shapes:
   - Cut the rolled-out dough into the desired shapes for your crackers using a knife or cookie cutter.
6. Transfer to Baking Sheet:
   - Gently place the cut crackers on a silicone baking mat or parchment paper-lined baking sheet.
7. Bake:
   - Bake in the preheated oven for about 15-20 minutes or until the crackers are firm and lightly browned.
8. Cool:
   - On a wire rack, let the crackers cool fully.
9. Serve:
   - Your flaxseed and parmesan crackers are ready to eat after they have cooled. Store any extras in an airtight container.

Nutritional Values: The quantity and dimensions of the crackers you manufacture will affect their nutritional content.

Spinach and Ricotta Stuffed Peppers

Time: 45 minutes
Preparation: 15 minutes
Cooking: 30 minutes
Servings: 4

INGREDIENTS

- 4 bell peppers (red, yellow, or green)
- 1 cup ricotta cheese
- 2 cups fresh spinach, chopped
- 1/2 cup mozzarella cheese, shredded
- 1/4 cup Parmesan cheese, grated
- 1/4 cup red onion, finely chopped
- 1 clove garlic, minced
- 1/2 teaspoon dried basil
- 1/2 teaspoon dried oregano
- Salt and black pepper, to taste
- Olive oil for drizzling

INSTRUCTIONS

1. Preheat Oven:
   - Set the oven temperature to 175°C, or 350°F.
2. Prepare Bell Peppers:
   - Remove the seeds and membranes from the bell peppers by cutting off the tops. Rinse them and set them aside.
3. Make Filling:
   - In a bowl, combine the ricotta cheese, chopped fresh spinach, shredded mozzarella cheese, grated Parmesan cheese, finely chopped red onion, minced garlic, dried basil, dried oregano, salt, and black pepper. Mix until the filling is well combined.
4. Stuff Peppers:
   - Carefully stuff each bell pepper with the spinach and ricotta mixture.
5. Arrange in Baking Dish:
   - The stuffed bell peppers should be put in a baking dish.
6. Drizzle with Olive Oil:
   - Drizzle the tops of the stuffed peppers with a bit of olive oil.
7. Bake:
   - Bake the baking dish in the preheated oven

for 25 to 30 minutes, or until the peppers are soft, covered with foil.

8. Serve:
   - Remove from the oven and serve your Spinach and Ricotta Stuffed Peppers as a nutritious and flavorful dish.

Nutritional Values (per serving, assuming 4 servings): Calories: 250 Kcal; Protein: 12g; Carbohydrates: 12g; Fat: 16g

Avocado and Strawberry Salad

Time: 15 minutes
Preparation: 15 minutes
Servings: 4

INGREDIENTS

- For the Salad:
- 4 cups mixed salad greens (e.g., spinach, arugula, or spring mix)
- 2 avocados, peeled, pitted, and sliced
- 2 cups strawberries, hulled and sliced
- 1/2 cup red onion, thinly sliced
- 1/4 cup pecans or walnuts, toasted and chopped
- 1/4 cup feta cheese, crumbled (optional)
- Black pepper, to taste
- For the Dressing:
- 3 tablespoons extra-virgin olive oil
- 2 tablespoons balsamic vinegar
- 1 tablespoon honey or maple syrup
- 1 teaspoon Dijon mustard
- Salt and black pepper, to taste

INSTRUCTIONS

For the Dressing:
1. Prepare Dressing:
   - In a small bowl, whisk together the extra-virgin olive oil, balsamic vinegar, honey or maple syrup, Black pepper, salt, and Dijon mustard. Discard the dressing.

For the Salad:
1. Assemble Salad Greens:
   - Divide the mixed salad greens evenly among four salad plates.

2. Arrange Avocado and Strawberries:
   - Arrange the sliced avocados and strawberries over the bed of greens.
3. Add Red Onion:
   - Sprinkle the thinly sliced red onion over the avocados and strawberries.
4. Top with Nuts and Cheese:
   - Sprinkle the toasted and chopped pecans or walnuts and crumbled feta cheese (if using) over the salad.
5. Drizzle with Dressing:
   - Cover the salad with a drizzle of the prepared dressing.
6. Season with Pepper:
   - Finish the salad by adding a pinch of black pepper for extra flavor.
7. Serve:
   - Serve your Avocado and Strawberry Salad immediately as a refreshing and nutritious dish.

Nutritional Values (per serving, assuming 4 servings): Calories: 250 Kcal; Protein: 4g; Carbohydrates: 20g; Fat: 19g

Zucchini Lasagna with Spinach and Ricotta

Time: 75 minutes
Preparation: 30 minutes
Cooking: 45 minutes
Servings: 6

INGREDIENTS

- For the Zucchini "Noodles":
- 4 medium zucchinis, thinly sliced lengthwise
- Olive oil for brushing
- Salt and black pepper, to taste
- For the Filling:
- 2 cups fresh spinach, chopped
- 2 cups ricotta cheese
- 1 cup mozzarella cheese, shredded
- 1/2 cup oParmesan cheese, grated
- 1 egg
- 1/2 teaspoon dried basil
- 1/2 teaspoon dried oregano
- Salt and black pepper, to taste
- For the Tomato Sauce:
- 2 cups tomato sauce (no added sugar)

- 1 clove garlic, minced
- 1/2 teaspoon dried basil
- 1/2 teaspoon dried oregano
- Salt and black pepper, to taste

INSTRUCTIONS

For the Zucchini "Noodles":
1. Preheat Oven:
   - Preheat your oven to 375°F (190°C).
2. Prepare Zucchini:
   - With a mandoline or sharp knife, finely slice the courgette lengthwise. Lay the slices on paper towels, sprinkle with salt, and let them sit for about 10 minutes to release excess moisture.
3. Brush and Roast:
   - Pat the zucchini slices dry, brush them lightly with olive oil, and roast in the preheated oven for about 10-15 minutes until they become tender.

For the Filling:
1. Prepare Filling:
   - In a bowl, combine the chopped fresh spinach, ricotta cheese, shredded mozzarella cheese, grated Parmesan cheese, egg, dried basil, dried oregano, salt, and black pepper. Mix well to create the filling.

For the Tomato Sauce:
1. Prepare Tomato Sauce:
   - In a saucepan, heat the tomato sauce, minced garlic, dried basil, dried oregano, salt, and black pepper. After a short while of simmering, turn off the heat.

Assembly:
1. Layer Lasagna:
   - In a baking dish, start by layering zucchini "noodles" at the bottom.
   - Spread the ricotta and spinach filling on top.
   - Repeat the layers until all ingredients are used, finishing with a layer of zucchini noodles on top.
2. Bake:
   - Bake the baking dish for about 30 minutes in a preheated oven, covered with foil. Remove the foil and bake for an additional 15 minutes or until the lasagna is hot and bubbly.
3. Serve:
   - Before serving, let the zucchini lasagna with

spinach and ricotta cool for a few minutes. Enjoy!

Nutritional Values (per serving, assuming 6 servings): Calories: 300 Kcal; Protein: 16g; Carbohydrates: 10g; Fat: 22g

Broccoli and Cheddar Fritters

Time: 30 minutes
Preparation: 15 minutes
Cooking: 15 minutes
Servings: 4

INGREDIENTS

- 2 cups broccoli florets, steamed and finely chopped
- 1 cup cheddar cheese, shredded
- 1/2 cup whole wheat flour (or almond flour for a gluten-free option)
- 2 eggs
- 1/4 cup red onion, finely chopped
- 2 cloves garlic, minced
- 1/2 teaspoon dried oregano
- 1/2 teaspoon dried thyme
- Salt and black pepper, to taste
- Olive oil, for frying

INSTRUCTIONS

1. Prepare Broccoli:
   - When the broccoli florets are tender, steam them. After steaming, cut them finely.
2. Mix Ingredients:
   - In a large mixing bowl, combine the chopped broccoli, cheddar cheese, whole wheat flour (or almond flour), eggs, finely chopped red onion, minced garlic, dried oregano, dried thyme, salt, and black pepper. Mix until all ingredients are well combined.
3. Form Fritters:
   - Using your hands, shape the mixture into fritters or patties. You have the freedom to customise their size to your liking.
4. Heat Oil:
   - Heat olive oil in a big skillet over medium heat.
5. Fry Fritters:
   - The fritters should be cooked for about 3–4

minutes on each side, or until they are crispy and golden brown, by carefully placing them in the hot skillet.

6. Drain and Serve:
   - Take out of the skillet the fritters and lay them on paper towels to absorb extra oil.
7. Serve:
   - Serve your hot broccoli and cheddar fritters as a tasty and wholesome side dish or snack.

Nutritional Values (per serving, assuming 4 servings): Calories: 250 Kcal; Protein: 12g; Carbohydrates: 15g; Fat: 16g

Creamy Coconut and Vegetable Curry

Time: 45 minutes
Preparation: 15 minutes
Cooking: 30 minutes
Servings: 4

INGREDIENTS

- For the Curry:
- 2 cups mixed vegetables (e.g., bell peppers, carrots, broccoli, and snap peas), chopped
- 1 cup cauliflower florets
- 1 cup green beans, chopped
- 1 can (14 ounces) coconut milk
- 2 tablespoons red curry paste
- 1 tablespoon coconut oil
- 1 small onion, chopped
- 2 cloves garlic, minced
- 1 tablespoon ginger, minced
- 1 tablespoon soy sauce or tamari
- 1 tablespoon honey or maple syrup
- Salt and black pepper, to taste
- Cilantro for garnish
- For Serving:
- Cooked rice or cauliflower rice (for a low-carb option)

INSTRUCTIONS

1. Sauté Aromatics:
   - In a large skillet or pan, heat the coconut oil over medium heat. Add the chopped onion, minced garlic, and minced ginger. They should become fragrant after a few minutes of sautéing.

2. Add Curry Paste:
   - To unleash the flavours, stir in the red curry paste and heat for one additional minute.
3. Add Vegetables:
   - Add the chopped mixed vegetables, cauliflower florets, and chopped green beans to the pan. Sauté for a few minutes until the vegetables start to soften.
4. Pour Coconut Milk:
   - Pour in the can of coconut milk, soy sauce or tamari, and honey or maple syrup. Stir to combine.
5. Simmer:
   - Reduce the heat to low, cover, and simmer the curry until the veggies are soft and the sauce has thickened, about 15 to 20 minutes.
6. Season:
   - To taste, add salt and black pepper for seasoning.
7. Serve:
   - Serve your Creamy Coconut and Vegetable Curry over cooked rice or cauliflower rice for a low-carb option.
8. Garnish:
   - Garnish with fresh cilantro before serving.

Nutritional Values (per serving, assuming 4 servings, excluding rice): Calories: 250 Kcal; Protein: 4g; Carbohydrates: 15g; Fat: 20g

Stuffed Eggplant with Walnut and Cheese

Time: 60 minutes
Preparation: 20 minutes
Cooking: 40 minutes
Servings: 4

INGREDIENTS

- For the Stuffed Eggplant:
- 2 large eggplants
- 1 cup walnuts, chopped
- 1 cup feta cheese, crumbled
- 1/2 cup fresh parsley, chopped
- 1/4 cup red onion, finely chopped
- 2 cloves garlic, minced
- 1/4 cup olive oil
- Salt and black pepper, to taste
- For the Tomato Sauce:

- 2 cups tomato sauce (no added sugar)
- 1 clove garlic, minced
- 1/2 teaspoon dried oregano
- Salt and black pepper, to taste

INSTRUCTIONS

For the Stuffed Eggplant:

1. Preheat Oven:
   - Preheat your oven to 375°F (190°C).
2. Prepare Eggplants:
   - Cut the tops off the eggplants and scoop out the flesh, leaving about a 1/2-inch thick shell. Chop the scooped-out eggplant flesh.
3. Sauté Eggplant:
   - In a skillet, heat the olive oil over medium heat. Add the minced garlic, finely chopped red onion, and chopped eggplant flesh. They should become fragrant after a few minutes of sautéing.
4. Prepare Filling:
   - In a bowl, combine the sautéed eggplant mixture with the chopped walnuts, crumbled feta cheese, chopped fresh parsley, salt, and black pepper. Mix well to create the filling.
5. Stuff Eggplants:
   - Stuff the hollowed eggplant shells with the walnut and cheese filling.
6. For the Tomato Sauce:
   - In a separate saucepan, heat the tomato sauce, minced garlic, dried oregano, salt, and black pepper. Simmer for a few minutes.
7. Bake:
   - Place the stuffed eggplants in a baking dish. Pour the tomato sauce over the stuffed eggplants.
8. Cover and Bake:
   - Bake the baking dish in the preheated oven for about thirty to thirty-five minutes, or until the eggplant shells are soft. Cover with foil.
9. Serve:
   - Serve your Stuffed Eggplant with Walnut and Cheese hot as a delicious and hearty dish.

Nutritional Values (per serving, assuming 4 servings): Calories: 350 Kcal; Protein: 10g; Carbohydrates: 20g; Fat: 26g

Asparagus and Goat Cheese Tart

Time: 60 minutes
Preparation: 15 minutes
Baking: 45 minutes
Servings: 4

INGREDIENTS

- For the Tart Crust:
- 1 cup all-purpose flour
- 1/2 cup whole wheat flour
- 1/2 cup cold butter, cubed
- 1/4 cup ice water
- 1/2 teaspoon salt
- For the Filling:
- 1 bunch of asparagus spears, trimmed
- 6 ounces goat cheese, crumbled
- 2 eggs
- 1/4 cup heavy cream
- 1/4 cup milk
- 1/4 cup fresh parsley, chopped
- 1 clove garlic, minced
- 1/2 teaspoon dried thyme
- Salt and black pepper, to taste
- Olive oil for drizzling

INSTRUCTIONS

For the Tart Crust:

1. Prepare Crust:
   - In a food processor, combine the all-purpose flour, whole wheat flour, cubed cold butter, and salt. Pulse until the mixture resembles coarse crumbs.
2. Add Water:
   - While the food processor is running, slowly drizzle in the ice water until the dough comes together.
3. Chill Dough:
   - Take out of the food processor the dough and form it into a disc. Refrigerate it for a minimum of half an hour after wrapping it in plastic wrap.

For the Filling:

1. Preheat Oven:
   - Preheat your oven to 375°F (190°C).

2. Blanch Asparagus:
   - Bring a pot of water to a boil. Blanch the trimmed asparagus spears for 1-2 minutes, then immediately transfer them to an ice water bath to stop the cooking. Drain and set aside.
3. Roll Out Dough:
   - The cold dough should be rolled out to fit a tart pan on a surface dusted with flour. After pressing the dough into the pan, cut off any extra.
4. Prepare Filling:
   - In a bowl, whisk together the eggs, heavy cream, milk, chopped fresh parsley, minced garlic, dried thyme, salt, and black pepper.
5. Assemble Tart:
   - Cover the bottom of the tart crust with the crumbled goat cheese. Top the cheese with the blanched asparagus spears. Pour the egg and cream mixture over the asparagus.
6. Drizzle with Olive Oil:
   - Drizzle the top with a bit of olive oil.
7. Bake:
   - Bake for 40 to 45 minutes, or until the tart is set and the crust is golden brown, in a preheated oven.
8. Cool and Serve:
   - Before slicing, let the asparagus and goat cheese tart cool for a few minutes. Serve warm or at room temperature.

Nutritional Values (per serving, assuming 4 servings): Calories: 450 Kcal; Protein: 12g; Carbohydrates: 30g; Fat: 32g

Chard and Feta Quiche

Time: 60 minutes
Preparation: 20 minutes
Baking: 40 minutes
Servings: 6

INGREDIENTS

- For the Quiche Crust:
- 1 cup all-purpose flour
- 1/2 cup whole wheat flour
- 1/2 cup cold butter, cubed
- 1/4 cup ice water
- 1/2 teaspoon salt
- For the Quiche Filling:
- 4 cups Swiss chard, stems removed, and leaves chopped
- 1 cup feta cheese, crumbled
- 4 eggs
- 1 cup milk
- 1/4 cup red onion, finely chopped
- 1 clove garlic, minced
- 1/4 teaspoon dried thyme
- Salt and black pepper, to taste
- Olive oil for sautéing

INSTRUCTIONS

For the Quiche Crust:
1. Prepare Crust:
   - In a food processor, combine the all-purpose flour, whole wheat flour, cubed cold butter, and salt. Pulse until the mixture resembles coarse crumbs.
2. Add Water:
   - Slowly pour in the ice water while the food processor is operating until the dough comes together.
3. Chill Dough:
   - Take out of the food processor the dough and form it into a disc. Refrigerate it for a minimum of half an hour after wrapping it in plastic wrap.

For the Quiche Filling:
1. Preheat Oven:
   - Preheat your oven to 375°F (190°C).
2. Sauté Chard:
   - Heat a little amount of olive oil in a skillet over medium heat. Sauté the chopped Swiss chard until it wilts, and most of the moisture has evaporated. Set aside.
3. Roll Out Dough:
   - Roll out the chilled dough to fit a pie or quiche dish on a lightly floured board. After pressing the dough into the dish, cut off any extra.
4. Prepare Filling:
   - In a bowl, whisk together the eggs, milk, finely chopped red onion, minced garlic, dried thyme, salt, and black pepper.
5. Assemble Quiche:
   - Spread the sautéed Swiss chard evenly over the quiche crust. Sprinkle the crumbled feta cheese on top.

6. Pour Egg Mixture:
   - Drizzle the feta and chard with the egg and milk mixture.
7. Bake:
   - Bake the Chard and Feta Quiche for 35 to 40 minutes, or until the crust is golden brown and the quiche is set.
8. Cool and Serve:
   - Before slicing, let the quiche cool for a few minutes. Heat or serve room temperature.

Nutritional Values (per serving, assuming 6 servings): Calories: 350 Kcal; Protein: 12g; Carbohydrates: 25g; Fat: 20g

Mushroom and Spinach Stroganoff with Coconut Cream

Time: 30 minutes
Preparation: 10 minutes
Cooking: 20 minutes
Servings: 4

INGREDIENTS

- 8 ounces mushrooms, sliced
- 4 cups spinach
- 1 small onion, finely chopped
- 2 cloves garlic, minced
- 1 can (14 ounces) coconut cream
- 2 tablespoons olive oil
- 1 tablespoon all-purpose flour (or gluten-free flour)
- 1 teaspoon paprika
- 1/2 teaspoon dried thyme
- Salt and black pepper, to taste
- Fresh parsley for garnish
- Cooked pasta or rice (for serving)

INSTRUCTIONS

1. Sauté Mushrooms:
   - Heat olive oil in a big skillet over medium heat. Add the sliced mushrooms and sauté for about 5-7 minutes, or until they release their moisture and become browned. Remove the mushrooms from the skillet and set aside.

2. Sauté Onion and Garlic:
   - In the same skillet, add the finely chopped onion and minced garlic. They should become fragrant after a few minutes of sautéing.
3. Add Flour and Spices:
   - Sprinkle the all-purpose flour (or gluten-free flour) over the onions and garlic. Stir to combine. Add the paprika, dried thyme, salt, and black pepper. Cook for another minute.
4. Pour Coconut Cream:
   - Pour in the can of coconut cream and stir to combine. Bring the mixture to a gentle simmer.
5. Add Spinach and Mushrooms:
   - Once the coconut cream mixture is simmering, add the spinach and sautéed mushrooms. Stir and cook until the spinach wilts and the sauce thickens, about 5 minutes.
6. Adjust Seasoning:
   - Taste and, if necessary, adjust the seasoning with more salt and pepper.
7. Serve:
   - Serve your Mushroom and Spinach Stroganoff over cooked pasta or rice. Garnish with fresh parsley.

Nutritional Values (per serving, assuming 4 servings, excluding pasta or rice): Calories: 300 Kcal; Protein: 5g; Carbohydrates: 10g; Fat: 27g

Cauliflower and Cheese Gratin

Time: 45 minutes
Preparation: 20 minutes
Baking: 25 minutes
Servings: 6

INGREDIENTS

- 1 large cauliflower head, cut into florets
- 2 cups cheddar cheese, shredded
- 1/2 cup Parmesan cheese, grated
- 2 cups heavy cream
- 2 cloves garlic, minced
- 1/2 teaspoon dried thyme
- Salt and black pepper, to taste
- Butter for greasing
- Fresh parsley for garnish

INSTRUCTIONS

1. Preheat Oven:
   - Preheat your oven to 375°F (190°C).
2. Steam Cauliflower:
   - Steam the cauliflower florets for five to seven minutes, or until they are soft. Empty and place aside.
3. Prepare Gratin Dish:
   - Grease a gratin or baking dish with butter.
4. Layer Cauliflower:
   - Arrange the steamed cauliflower florets in the prepared dish.
5. Make Cheese Sauce:
   - In a saucepan, heat the heavy cream over medium heat. Add the minced garlic, dried thyme, salt, and black pepper. Stir until it's heated but not boiling.
6. Add Cheese:
   - Remove the cream mixture from the heat and stir in 1.5 cups of the shredded cheddar cheese and the grated Parmesan cheese. Stir until the cheese is melted and the sauce is smooth.
7. Pour Over Cauliflower:
   - Pour the cheese sauce over the cauliflower into the dish, making sure the cauliflower is well coated.
8. Top with Cheese:
   - Sprinkle the remaining 0.5 cups of shredded cheddar cheese over the top.
9. Bake:
   - Bake, stirring every 5 to 10 minutes to ensure equal baking, in a preheated oven for about 20 minutes, or until golden brown.
10. Garnish:
    - Garnish with fresh parsley before serving.

Nutritional Values (per serving, assuming 6 servings): Calories: 450 Kcal; Protein: 15g; Carbohydrates: 8g; Fat: 40g

Avocado and Almond Butter Toast on Flaxseed Bread

Time: 10 minutes
Preparation: 5 minutes
Servings: 2

INGREDIENTS

- 2 slices of flaxseed bread (or any low-carb bread of your choice)
- 1 ripe avocado
- 4 tablespoons almond butter
- Chia seeds (for garnish, optional)
- Red pepper flakes (for garnish, optional)
- Salt and black pepper, to taste

INSTRUCTIONS

1. Toast the Bread:
   - Toast the slices of flaxseed bread until they are crispy and golden brown.
2. Prepare Avocado:
   - Scoop the flesh into a bowl after slicing the ripe avocado in half and removing the pit.. Mash it with a fork and to taste, add a dash of salt and black pepper for seasoning.
3. Spread Almond Butter:
   - Toast each slice of bread and spread 2 teaspoons of almond butter on it.
4. Add Mashed Avocado:
   - Spread the mashed avocado on top of the almond butter.
5. Garnish:
   - Optionally, you can garnish your Avocado and Almond Butter Toast with a sprinkle of chia seeds for added texture and red pepper flakes for a hint of heat.
6. Serve:
   - Serve your toast with avocado and almond butter as a filling and healthy breakfast or snack..

Nutritional Values (per serving, assuming 2 servings): Calories: 350 Kcal; Protein: 9g; Carbohydrates: 20g; Fat: 28g

Spinach and Artichoke Dip with Vegetable Sticks

Time: 30 minutes
Preparation: 10 minutes
Cooking: 20 minutes
Servings: 4

INGREDIENTS

- For the Dip:
- 8 ounces spinach, chopped
- 1 can (14 ounces) artichoke hearts, drained and chopped
- 1 cup cream cheese
- 1/2 cup sour cream
- 1/2 cup mayonnaise
- 1 cup shredded mozzarella cheese
- 1/2 cup grated Parmesan cheese
- 2 cloves garlic, minced
- 1/2 teaspoon dried basil
- 1/2 teaspoon dried oregano
- Salt and black pepper, to taste
- Olive oil for sautéing
- For the Vegetable Sticks:
- Carrot sticks
- Cucumber sticks
- Bell pepper strips
- Celery sticks
- Cherry tomatoes

INSTRUCTIONS

For the Dip:

1. Preheat Oven:
   - Preheat your oven to 375°F (190°C).
2. Sauté Spinach:
   - Heat a little amount of olive oil in a skillet over medium heat. Sauté the chopped spinach until it wilts. Remove from heat and set aside.
3. Prepare the Dip:
   - In a mixing bowl, combine the sautéed spinach, chopped artichoke hearts, cream cheese, sour cream, mayonnaise, shredded mozzarella cheese, grated Parmesan cheese, minced garlic, dried basil, dried oregano, salt, and black pepper. Mix well.
4. Bake:
   - Transfer the dip mixture to an oven-safe dish. Bake in the preheated oven for about 20-25 minutes or until the top is bubbly and lightly browned.

For the Vegetable Sticks:

1. Prepare Vegetables:
   - Wash and cut carrot sticks, cucumber sticks, bell pepper strips, celery sticks, and halve cherry tomatoes.
2. Serve:
   - Arrange the vegetable sticks around the hot Spinach and Artichoke Dip and serve as a delightful and wholesome appetizer.

Nutritional Values (per serving, assuming 4 servings, excluding vegetables): Calories: 350 Kcal; Protein: 12g; Carbohydrates: 8g; Fat: 28g

Cucumber and Cream Cheese Roll-Ups

Time: 10 minutes
Preparation: 10 minutes
Servings: 2

INGREDIENTS

- 1 large cucumber
- 4 ounces of cream cheese
- 1 teaspoon fresh dill, chopped
- 1/2 teaspoon fresh chives, chopped
- Salt and black pepper, to taste

INSTRUCTIONS

1. Prepare Cucumber:
   - Wash the cucumber thoroughly. You can peel it if you prefer or leave the skin on for added texture and nutrients.
2. Slice Cucumber:
   - Using a knife or mandoline slicer, cut the cucumber lengthwise into thin, long slices. Slices should ideally be about 1/8 inch thick.
3. Prepare Cream Cheese Mixture:
   - In a bowl, combine the cream cheese, fresh dill, fresh chives, salt, and black pepper. Mix well to create a creamy herb spread.
4. Spread Cream Cheese:
- Lay down each slice of cucumber and cover the

whole surface with a thin layer of the herb cream cheese mixture.

5. Roll Up:
   - Carefully roll up each cucumber slice, starting from one end, to create little roll-ups. You can secure them with toothpicks if needed.
6. Serve:
   - Arrange your Cucumber and Cream Cheese Roll-Ups on a serving platter. You can garnish them with additional herbs or a dash of black pepper if desired.

Nutritional Values (per serving, assuming 2 servings): Calories: 120 Kcal; Protein: 2g; Carbohydrates: 6g; Fat: 10g

Vegetable and Cheese Platter with Olive Tapenade

Time: 15 minutes
Preparation: 15 minutes
Servings: 4

INGREDIENTS

- For the Vegetable and Cheese Platter:
- A variety of vegetables, such as cherry tomatoes, cucumber slices, carrot sticks, bell pepper strips, and celery sticks
- A selection of cheeses, such as cheddar, brie, and goat cheese
- Grapes and berries for sweetness
- Nuts, such as almonds and walnuts, for added crunch
- Olives for extra flavor
- For the Olive Tapenade:
- 1 cup pitted black olives
- 2 cloves garlic, minced
- 1 tablespoon capers
- 2 tablespoons extra-virgin olive oil
- 1 teaspoon lemon juice
- 1 teaspoon fresh thyme leaves (or 1/2 teaspoon dried)
- Freshly ground black pepper, to taste

INSTRUCTIONS

For the Vegetable and Cheese Platter:
1. Prepare Vegetables:
   - Wash and cut the vegetables into bite-sized pieces, such as cherry tomatoes, cucumber slices, carrot sticks, bell pepper strips, and celery sticks. Arrange them on a platter.
2. Cheese Selection:
   - Arrange a variety of cheeses, such as cheddar, brie, and goat cheese, alongside the vegetables on the platter.
3. Add Fruits and Nuts:
   - Add grapes and berries for sweetness and nuts, such as almonds and walnuts, for added crunch.
4. Include Olives:
   - Place a bowl of olives on the platter for extra flavor.

For the Olive Tapenade:
1. Prepare Tapenade:
   - In a food processor, combine the pitted black olives, minced garlic, capers, extra-virgin olive oil, lemon juice, and fresh thyme leaves. Pulse just long enough to incorporate all of the ingredients, leaving some chunks for texture.
2. Season:
   - Season the olive tapenade with freshly ground black pepper to taste. Adjust the flavors to your liking.
3. Serve:
   - Transfer the olive tapenade to a small bowl and place it on the Vegetable and Cheese Platter.

Nutritional Values (for the entire platter, divided by 4 servings): Calories: Varies depending on the quantity of vegetables, cheese, and olives; Protein: Varies; Carbohydrates: Varies; Fat: Varies

Grilled Vegetable Salad with Feta Crumble

Time: 30 minutes
Preparation: 15 minutes
Grilling: 15 minutes
Servings: 4

INGREDIENTS

- For the Salad:
- A variety of vegetables, such as zucchini, red bell pepper, yellow bell pepper, eggplant, and cherry tomatoes
- Olive oil for brushing
- Salt and black pepper, to taste
- Mixed greens, such as spinach and arugula
- 4 ounces feta cheese, crumbled
- For the Dressing:
- 3 tablespoons extra-virgin olive oil
- 2 tablespoons balsamic vinegar
- 1 teaspoon Dijon mustard
- 1 clove garlic, minced
- 1 teaspoon honey (optional)
- Salt and black pepper, to taste

INSTRUCTIONS

For the Grilled Vegetable Salad:

1. Preheat Grill:
   - Set your grill's temperature to medium-high.
2. Prepare Vegetables:
   - Wash and slice the vegetables for grilling, such as zucchini, red bell pepper, yellow bell pepper, eggplant, and cherry tomatoes.
3. Brush with Olive Oil:
   - Brush the sliced vegetables with olive oil and season them with salt and black pepper.
4. Grill Vegetables:
   - Arrange the veggies on the grill and cook, rotating regularly, for 10 to 15 minutes, or until they are soft and marked with grill marks. Remove from the grill and let them cool slightly.
5. Assemble Salad:
   - On a serving platter, arrange a bed of mixed greens. Top with the grilled vegetables.

For the Dressing:

1. Prepare Dressing:
   - In a small bowl, whisk together the extra-virgin olive oil, balsamic vinegar, Dijon mustard, minced garlic, honey (if using), salt, and black pepper.
2. Drizzle Dressing:
   - Drizzle the dressing over the Grilled Vegetable Salad.
3. Add Feta Crumble:
   - Sprinkle the crumbled feta cheese over the top of the salad.
4. Serve:
   - Serve your Grilled Vegetable Salad with Feta Crumble as a flavorful and nutritious dish.

Nutritional Values (per serving, assuming 4 servings): Calories: Varies depending on the quantity and types of vegetables used; Protein: Varies; Carbohydrates: Varies; Fat: Varies

Baked Avocado with Egg and Chives

Time: 25 minutes
Preparation: 10 minutes
Baking: 15 minutes
Servings: 2

INGREDIENTS

- 2 avocados
- 2 eggs
- 1 tablespoon fresh chives, chopped
- Salt and black pepper, to taste
- Olive oil for drizzling
- Cherry tomatoes (optional, for garnish)

INSTRUCTIONS

1. Preheat Oven:
   - Preheat your oven to 375°F (190°C).
2. Prepare Avocados:
   - Cut the avocados in half and remove the pits. Scoop out a bit of the flesh from each avocado half to create a larger cavity for the egg. Be careful not to remove too much.
3. Place Avocados:
   - Place the avocado halves in a baking dish so they are stable and won't tip over.

4. Crack Eggs:
   - In each half of an avocado, crack one egg. Season the eggs with salt and black pepper.
5. Bake:
   - Bake the eggs and avocado in a preheated oven for fifteen minutes or so, or until the yolks are still little runny but the egg whites are set.
6. Garnish:
   - Sprinkle fresh chives over the baked avocados. If desired, you can garnish with halved cherry tomatoes for added color and flavor.
7. Serve:
   - Serve your Baked Avocado with Egg and Chives as a nutritious and delicious dish. You can enjoy it as is or with a side of whole-grain toast or a mixed greens salad.

Nutritional Values (per serving, assuming 2 servings): Calories: 250 Kcal; Protein: 8g; Carbohydrates: 9g; Fat: 20g

Caprese Salad with Olive Oil and Basil

Time: 15 minutes
Preparation: 15 minutes
Servings: 4

INGREDIENTS

- 4 large ripe tomatoes
- 8 ounces of fresh mozzarella cheese
- Fresh basil leaves
- Extra-virgin olive oil
- Balsamic vinegar (optional)
- Salt and black pepper, to taste

INSTRUCTIONS

1. Prepare Tomatoes:
   - Wash the tomatoes and cut them into thick slices.
2. Slice Mozzarella:
- Cut the fresh mozzarella cheese into pieces that are about the same size as the tomatoes.
3. Arrange Caprese Salad:
   - On a serving platter, alternate the tomato slices, mozzarella cheese slices, and fresh basil leaves. Create a visually appealing pattern.
4. Drizzle with Olive Oil:
   - Drizzle extra-virgin olive oil generously over the Caprese Salad. You can also add a drizzle of balsamic vinegar for extra flavor if desired.
5. Season:
   - Toss in a little salt and freshly ground black pepper, to taste, to dress the salad.
6. Serve:
   - Serve your Caprese Salad with Olive Oil and Basil as a classic and refreshing dish. It's best served immediately.

Nutritional Values (per serving, assuming 4 servings): Calories: Varies depending on the quantity of ingredients; Protein: Varies; Carbohydrates: Varies; Fat: Varies

Avocado and Spinach Green Smoothie

Time: 10 minutes
Preparation: 10 minutes
Servings: 2

INGREDIENTS

- 1 ripe avocado
- 2 cups fresh spinach leaves
- 1 banana
- 1 cup almond milk (or any milk of your choice)
- 1/2 cup Greek yogurt
- 1 tablespoon honey (optional for sweetness)
- Ice cubes (optional for a colder smoothie)

INSTRUCTIONS

1. Prepare Ingredients:
- Remove the pit from the ripe avocado, cut it in half, and scoop the flesh into a blender. Add the fresh spinach leaves.
2. Add Banana:
   - Peel the banana and add it to the blender.
3. Include Almond Milk:
   - Pour in the almond milk (or your preferred milk).
4. Add Greek Yogurt:
   - Spoon the Greek yogurt into the blender.
5. Sweeten (Optional):
   - If you prefer a sweeter smoothie, you can add a tablespoon of honey.
6. Blend:
   - Blend all the ingredients until the mixture is smooth and creamy.
7. Serve:
   - Pour your Avocado and Spinach Green Smoothie into glasses and serve immediately.

Nutritional Values (per serving, assuming 2 servings): Calories: 250 Kcal; Protein: 6g; Carbohydrates: 28g; Fat: 15g

Mixed Berry and Coconut Milk Smoothie

Time: 10 minutes
Preparation: 10 minutes
Servings: 2

INGREDIENTS

- 2 cups mixed berries (strawberries, blueberries, raspberries)
- 1 cup coconut milk (unsweetened)
- 1 banana
- 1 tablespoon honey (optional for sweetness)
- Chia seeds (for garnish, optional)
- Ice cubes (optional for a colder smoothie)

INSTRUCTIONS

1. Prepare Ingredients:
   - Wash and prepare the mixed berries. Peel the banana.
2. Combine Ingredients:
   - In a blender, add the mixed berries, coconut milk, banana, and the optional tablespoon of honey for sweetness.
3. Blend:
   - Mix all the ingredients in a blender until the mixture is creamy and smooth.
4. Garnish (Optional):
   - If desired, you can sprinkle chia seeds on top for added texture and nutrition.
5. Serve:
   - Immediately serve your Mixed Berry and Coconut Milk Smoothie by pouring it into glasses.

Nutritional Values (per serving, assuming 2 servings): Calories: 250 Kcal; Protein: 3g; Carbohydrates: 40g; Fat: 10g

Almond Butter and Chia Seed Smoothie

Time: 10 minutes
Preparation: 10 minutes
Servings: 2

INGREDIENTS

- 2 cups almond milk (unsweetened)
- 2 tablespoons almond butter
- 2 tablespoons chia seeds
- 1 banana
- 1 tablespoon honey (optional for sweetness)
- Ice cubes (optional for a colder smoothie)

INSTRUCTIONS

1. Prepare Ingredients:
   - Peel the banana.
2. Combine Ingredients:
   - In a blender, add the almond milk, almond butter, chia seeds, and the peeled banana.
3. Blend:
   - Blend all the ingredients until the mixture is smooth and creamy. Add some ice cubes and blend them in if you want your smoothie to be colder.
4. Serve:
   - Fill glasses with your Chia Seed and Almond Butter Smoothie and serve right away.

Nutritional Values (per serving, assuming 2 servings): Calories: 220 Kcal; Protein: 6g; Carbohydrates: 25g; Fat: 12g

Blueberry and Walnut Protein Smoothie

Time: 10 minutes
Preparation: 10 minutes
Servings: 2

INGREDIENTS

- 2 cups blueberries (fresh or frozen)
- 1/2 cup walnuts
- 1 cup Greek yogurt
- 1 cup almond milk (unsweetened)
- 1 tablespoon honey (optional for sweetness)

- 1 scoop protein powder (flavor of your choice)
- Ice cubes (optional for a colder smoothie)

INSTRUCTIONS

1. Prepare Ingredients:
   - If using fresh blueberries, wash and rinse them. If you are using frozen blueberries, you can use them directly.
2. Combine Ingredients:
   - In a blender, add the blueberries, walnuts, Greek yogurt, almond milk, and the optional tablespoon of honey for sweetness.
3. Blend:
   - Add some ice cubes and blend them in if you want your smoothie to be colder.
4. Serve:
   - Transfer your protein smoothie with walnuts and blueberries into glasses and serve right away.

Nutritional Values (per serving, assuming 2 servings): Calories: 350 Kcal; Protein: 15g; Carbo-hydrates: 30g; Fat: 20g

Strawberry and Cream Smoothie with Flaxseeds

Time: 10 minutes
Preparation: 10 minutes
Servings: 2

INGREDIENTS

- 2 cups strawberries (fresh or frozen)
- 1 cup Greek yogurt
- 1 cup almond milk (unsweetened)
- 2 tablespoons flaxseeds
- 1 tablespoon honey (optional for sweetness)
- Ice cubes (optional for a colder smoothie)

INSTRUCTIONS

1. Prepare Ingredients:
   - If using fresh strawberries, wash and remove the green tops. If you are using frozen strawberries, you can use them directly.
2. Combine Ingredients:
   - In a blender, add the strawberries, Greek yogurt, almond milk, flaxseeds, and the optional tablespoon of honey for sweetness.

3. Blend:
   - Mix all the ingredients in a blender until the mixture is creamy and smooth. Add some ice cubes and blend them in if you want your smoothie to be colder.
4. Serve:
   - Fill glasses with your strawberry-cream smoothie including flaxseeds, then serve right away.

Nutritional Values (per serving, assuming 2 servings): Calories: 200 Kcal; Protein: 10g; Carbo-hydrates: 20g; Fat: 10g

Chocolate and Avocado Keto Smoothie

Time: 10 minutes
Preparation: 10 minutes
Servings: 2

INGREDIENTS

- 1 ripe avocado
- 2 tablespoons unsweetened cocoa powder
- 1 cup coconut milk (unsweetened)
- 1 cup almond milk (unsweetened)
- 2 tablespoons almond butter
- 1 tablespoon chia seeds
- 1 tablespoon erythritol or stevia (optional for sweetness)
- Ice cubes (optional for a colder smoothie)

INSTRUCTIONS

1. Prepare Ingredients:
   - Cut the ripe avocado in half, remove the pit, and scoop the flesh into a blender.
2. Combine Ingredients:
   - To the blender, add the unsweetened cocoa powder, coconut milk, almond milk, almond butter, chia seeds, and the optional sweetener (erythritol or stevia).
3. Blend:
   - Mix all the ingredients in a blender until the mixture is creamy and smooth. Add some ice cubes and blend them in if you want your smoothie to be colder.

4. Serve:
   - Transfer your Avocado and Chocolate Keto Smoothie into glasses and serve right away.

Nutritional Values (per serving, assuming 2 servings): Calories: 250 Kcal; Protein: 5g; Carbohydrates: 10g

Fiber: 8g; Fat: 22g

Cucumber and Mint Refreshing Smoothie

Time: 10 minutes
Preparation: 10 minutes
Servings: 2

INGREDIENTS

- 2 cucumbers, peeled and chopped
- 1 cup fresh mint leaves
- 1 cup Greek yogurt
- 1 cup almond milk (unsweetened)
- 1 tablespoon honey (optional for sweetness)
- Ice cubes (optional for a colder smoothie)

INSTRUCTIONS

1. Prepare Ingredients:
   - Peel and chop the cucumbers.
2. Combine Ingredients:
   - In a blender, add the chopped cucumbers, fresh mint leaves, Greek yogurt, almond milk, and the optional tablespoon of honey for sweetness.
3. Blend:
   - Mix all the ingredients in a blender until the mixture is creamy and smooth. Add some ice cubes and blend them in if you want your smoothie to be colder.
4. Serve:
   - Immediately serve your refreshing smoothie made with cucumber and mint by pouring it into glasses.

Nutritional Values (per serving, assuming 2 servings): Calories: 150 Kcal; Protein: 6g; Carbohydrates: 15g; Fat: 7g

Raspberry and Coconut Cream Smoothie

Time: 10 minutes
Preparation: 10 minutes
Servings: 2

INGREDIENTS

- 2 cups raspberries (fresh or frozen)
- 1 cup coconut milk (unsweetened)
- 1 cup Greek yogurt
- 2 tablespoons shredded coconut (unsweetened)
- 1 tablespoon honey (optional for sweetness)
- Ice cubes (optional for a colder smoothie)

INSTRUCTIONS

1. Prepare Ingredients:
   - If using fresh raspberries, wash and rinse them. If using frozen raspberries, you can use them directly.
2. Combine Ingredients:
   - In a blender, add the raspberries, coconut milk, Greek yogurt, shredded coconut, and the optional tablespoon of honey for sweetness.
3. Blend:
   - Mix all the ingredients in a blender until the mixture is creamy and smooth. Add some ice cubes and blend them in if you want your smoothie to be colder.
4. Serve:
   - Immediately serve your raspberry and coconut cream smoothie by pouring it into glasses.

Nutritional Values (per serving, assuming 2 servings): Calories: 250 Kcal; Protein: 6g; Carbohydrates: 20g; Fat: 15g

Kale and Almond Smoothie with Lemon Zest

Time: 10 minutes
Preparation: 10 minutes
Servings: 2

INGREDIENTS

- 2 cups fresh kale leaves
- 1/2 cup almonds
- 1 banana
- 1 lemon (zest and juice)
- 1 cup almond milk (unsweetened)
- 1 tablespoon honey (optional for sweetness)
- Ice cubes (optional for a colder smoothie)

INSTRUCTIONS

1. Prepare Ingredients:
   - Wash the fresh kale leaves and remove any tough stems. Peel the banana.
2. Combine Ingredients:
   - In a blender, add the kale leaves, almonds, peeled banana, the zest and juice of the lemon, almond milk, and the optional tablespoon of honey for sweetness.
3. Blend:
   - Mix all the ingredients in a blender until the mixture is creamy and smooth. Add some ice cubes and blend them in if you want your smoothie to be colder.
4. Serve:
   - Pour your Kale and Almond Smoothie with Lemon Zest into glasses and serve it immediately.

Nutritional Values (per serving, assuming 2 servings): Calories: 250 Kcal; Protein: 7g; Carbohydrates: 25g; Fat: 15g

Spinach and Blueberry Detox Smoothie

Time: 10 minutes
Preparation: 10 minutes
Servings: 2

INGREDIENTS

- 2 cups fresh spinach leaves
- 1 cup blueberries (fresh or frozen)
- 1 banana
- 1 cup almond milk (unsweetened)
- 1 tablespoon chia seeds
- 1 tablespoon honey (optional for sweetness)
- Ice cubes (optional for a colder smoothie)

INSTRUCTIONS

1. Prepare Ingredients:
   - Wash and rinse the fresh spinach leaves. If using fresh blueberries, wash them and remove any stems. If you are using frozen blueberries, you can use them directly. Peel the banana.
2. Combine Ingredients:
   - In a blender, add the spinach leaves, blueberries, peeled banana, almond milk, chia seeds, and the optional tablespoon of honey for sweetness.
3. Blend:
   - Mix all the ingredients in a blender until the mixture is creamy and smooth. Add some ice cubes and blend them in if you want your smoothie to be colder.
4. Serve:
   - Immediately serve your spinach and blueberry detox smoothie by pouring it into glasses.

Nutritional Values (per serving, assuming 2 servings): Calories: 200 Kcal; Protein: 5g; Carbohydrates: 35g; Fat: 6g

Tropical Coconut and Berry Blast

Time: 10 minutes
Preparation: 10 minutes
Servings: 2

INGREDIENTS

- 1 cup mixed berries (strawberries, blueberries, raspberries)
- 1/2 cup shredded coconut (unsweetened)
- 1 cup coconut milk (unsweetened)
- 1 banana
- 1 tablespoon honey (optional for sweetness)
- Ice cubes (optional for a colder smoothie)

INSTRUCTIONS

1. Prepare Ingredients:
   - If using fresh berries, wash and rinse them. If using frozen berries, you can use them directly. Peel the banana.
2. Combine Ingredients:
   - In a blender, add the mixed berries, shredded coconut, coconut milk, peeled banana, and the optional tablespoon of honey for sweetness.
3. Blend:
   - Mix all the ingredients in a blender until the mixture is creamy and smooth. Add some ice cubes and blend them in if you want your smoothie to be colder.
4. Serve:
   - Immediately serve your Tropical Coconut and Berry Blast by pouring it into glasses.

Nutritional Values (per serving, assuming 2 servings): Calories: 250 Kcal; Protein: 3g; Carbohydrates: 30g; Fat: 15g

Cacao and Macadamia Nut Creamy Smoothie

Time: 10 minutes
Preparation: 10 minutes
Servings: 2

INGREDIENTS

- 2 tablespoons raw cacao powder
- 1/2 cup macadamia nuts
- 2 cups almond milk (unsweetened)
- 1 banana
- 1 tablespoon honey (optional for sweetness)
- Ice cubes (optional for a colder smoothie)

INSTRUCTIONS

1. Prepare Ingredients:
   - If using whole macadamia nuts, boil them for a few minutes to soften them.
2. Combine Ingredients:
   - In a blender, add the raw cacao powder, the soaked or softened macadamia nuts, c almond milk, the peeled banana, and the optional tablespoon of honey for sweetness.
3. Blend:
   - Mix all the ingredients in a blender until the mixture is creamy and smooth. Add some ice cubes and blend them in if you want your smoothie to be colder.
4. Serve:
   - Immediately serve your chocolate and macadamia nut creamy smoothie by pouring it into glasses.

Nutritional Values (per serving, assuming 2 servings): Calories: 300 Kcal; Protein: 6g; Carbohydrates: 30g; Fat: 20g

Avocado and Lime Digestive Smoothie

Time: 10 minutes
Preparation: 10 minutes
Servings: 2

INGREDIENTS

- 1 ripe avocado
- Juice of 2 limes
- 1 cup Greek yogurt
- 1 cup almond milk (unsweetened)
- 1 tablespoon honey (optional for sweetness)
- Ice cubes (optional for a colder smoothie)
- Mint leaves (for garnish, optional)

INSTRUCTIONS

1. Prepare Ingredients:
   - Scoop the flesh into a blender after slicing the ripe avocado in half and removing the pit. Press the limes.
2. Combine Ingredients:
   - To the blender, add the avocado, lime juice, Greek yogurt, almond milk, and the optional tablespoon of honey for sweetness.
3. Blend:
   - Mix all the ingredients in a blender until the mixture is creamy and smooth. Add some ice cubes and blend them in if you want your smoothie to be colder.
4. Serve:
   - Pour your Avocado and Lime Digestive Smoothie into glasses. If desired, garnish with mint leaves and serve it immediately.

Nutritional Values (per serving, assuming 2 servings): Calories: 250 Kcal; Protein: 7g; Carbohydrates: 20g; Fat: 15g

Chia and Berry Antioxidant Smoothie

Time: 10 minutes
Preparation: 10 minutes
Servings: 2

INGREDIENTS

- 2 cups mixed berries (strawberries, blueberries, raspberries)
- 2 tablespoons chia seeds
- 1 cup Greek yogurt
- 1 cup almond milk (unsweetened)
- 1 tablespoon honey (optional for sweetness)
- Ice cubes (optional for a colder smoothie)

INSTRUCTIONS

1. Prepare Ingredients:
   - If using fresh berries, wash and rinse them. If using frozen berries, you can use them directly.
2. Combine Ingredients:
   - In a blender, add the mixed berries, chia seeds, Greek yogurt, almond milk, and the optional tablespoon of honey for sweetness.
3. Blend:
   - Mix all the ingredients in a blender until the mixture is creamy and smooth. Add some ice cubes and blend them in if you want your smoothie to be colder.
4. Serve:
   - Immediately serve your Chia and Berry Antioxidant Smoothie by pouring it into glasses.

Nutritional Values (per serving, assuming 2 servings): Calories: 250 Kcal; Protein: 8g; Carbohydrates: 30g; Fat: 10g

Spinach, Cucumber, and Ginger Zing Smoothie

Time: 10 minutes
Preparation: 10 minutes
Servings: 2

INGREDIENTS

- 2 cups fresh spinach leaves
- 1 cucumber, peeled and chopped
- 1-inch piece of ginger, peeled and grated
- Juice of 2 limes
- 1 cup coconut water (unsweetened)
- 1 tablespoon honey (optional for sweetness)
- Ice cubes (optional for a colder smoothie)
- Mint leaves (for garnish, optional)

INSTRUCTIONS

1. Prepare Ingredients:
   - Wash and rinse the fresh spinach leaves. Peel and chop the cucumber. Peel and grate the ginger. Juice the limes.
2. Combine Ingredients:
   - In a blender, add the spinach leaves, chopped cucumber, grated ginger, lime juice, coconut water, and the optional tablespoon of honey for sweetness.
3. Blend:
   - Mix all the ingredients in a blender until the mixture is creamy and smooth. Add some ice cubes and blend them in if you want your smoothie to be colder.
4. Serve:
   - Pour your Spinach, Cucumber, and Ginger Zing Smoothie into glasses. If desired, garnish with mint leaves and serve it immediately.

Nutritional Values (per serving, assuming 2 servings): Calories: 100 Kcal; Protein: 2g; Carbohydrates: 20g; Fat: 1g

Strawberry, Basil, and Coconut Fusion

Time: 10 minutes
Preparation: 10 minutes
Servings: 2

INGREDIENTS

- 2 cups strawberries (fresh or frozen)
- 1/2 cup fresh basil leaves
- 1 cup coconut milk (unsweetened)
- 1 tablespoon honey (optional for sweetness)
- Ice cubes (optional for a colder smoothie)

INSTRUCTIONS

1. Prepare Ingredients:
   - If using fresh strawberries, wash and rinse them. If you are using frozen strawberries, you can use them directly. Wash and pat dry the fresh basil leaves.
2. Combine Ingredients:
   - In a blender, add the strawberries, fresh basil leaves, coconut milk, and the optional tablespoon of honey for sweetness.
3. Blend:
   - Mix all the ingredients in a blender until the mixture is creamy and smooth. Add some ice cubes and blend them in if you want your smoothie to be colder.
4. Serve:
- Immediately serve your Coconut, Basil, and Strawberry Fusion by pouring it into glasses.

Nutritional Values (per serving, assuming 2 servings): Calories: 200 Kcal; Protein: 3g; Carbohydrates: 25g; Fat: 11g

Creamy Vanilla and Mixed Nut Smoothie

Time: 10 minutes
Preparation: 10 minutes
Servings: 2

INGREDIENTS

- 2 cups mixed nuts (almonds, walnuts, and macadamia nuts)
- 2 cups almond milk (unsweetened)
- 2 teaspoons vanilla extract
- 1 tablespoon honey (optional for sweetness)
- Ice cubes (optional for a colder smoothie)

INSTRUCTIONS

1. Prepare Ingredients:
   - If using whole mixed nuts, you can either soak them in water overnight or boil them for a few minutes to soften them.
2. Combine Ingredients:
   - In a blender, add the softened or soaked mixed nuts, almond milk, vanilla extract, and the optional tablespoon of honey for sweetness.
3. Blend:
   - Mix all the ingredients in a blender until the mixture is creamy and smooth. Add some ice cubes and blend them in if you want your smoothie to be colder.
4. Serve:
   - Pour your Creamy Vanilla and Mixed Nut Smoothie into glasses and serve it immediately.

Nutritional Values (per serving, assuming 2 servings): Calories: 350 Kcal; Protein: 8g; Carbohydrates: 15g; Fat: 30g

Meal Plan 28 days

Week 1

DAY	BREAKFAST	LUNCH	DINNER	SNACK	DESSERT
1	Spinach and Feta Omelets	Grilled Chicken Caesar Salad with Kale and Homemade Dressing	Herb Roasted Chicken with Brussels Sprouts	Avocado and Tuna Salad Cups	Avocado and Spinach Green Smoothie
2	Coconut Yogurt with Mixed Berries	Broccoli and Cheddar Soup	Lamb Chops with Mint Pesto and Asparagus	Spinach and Feta Stuffed Mushrooms	Mixed Berry and Coconut Milk Smoothie
3	Kale and Avocado Scrambled Eggs	Spinach and Avocado Salad with Olive Oil Dressing	Cauliflower Pizza with Cheese and Veggies	Baked Kale Chips with Sea Salt	Almond Butter and Chia Seed Smoothie
4	Zucchini Pancakes with Butter	Zucchini Noodle and Prawn Aglio Olio	Thai Coconut Fish Curry with Zucchini Noodles	Macadamia Nut Clusters with Dark Chocolate	Blueberry and Walnut Protein Smoothie
5	Asparagus and Cheese Frittata	Beef Lettuce Wraps with Cucumber Slaw	Pork Ribs with Kale Slaw	Coconut Milk Berry Popsicles	Strawberry and Cream Smoothie with Flaxseeds
6	Broccoli and Chicken Sausage Breakfast Casserole	Asparagus and Goat Cheese Quiche	Garlic Butter Shrimp with Broccoli Rice	Cucumber and Salmon Bite-sized Sandwiches	Chocolate and Avocado Keto Smoothie
7	Flaxseed Breakfast Porridge with Almond Milk	Seared Tuna Salad with Mixed Greens	Grilled Steak with Chimichurri and Spinach Salad	Chia Seed and Coconut Milk Pudding	Cucumber and Mint Refreshing Smoothie

Week 2

DAY	BREAKFAST	LUNCH	DINNER	SNACK	DESSERT
8	Coconut Flour Waffles	Lamb Kofta with Tzatziki Sauce	Chicken Zoodle Soup	Zucchini and Parmesan Crisps	Raspberry and Coconut Cream Smoothie
9	Coconut and Blueberry Muffins	Coconut Milk and Chicken Curry Soup	Beef Stew with Root Vegetables	Egg and Spinach Muffins	Kale and Almond Smoothie with Lemon Zest
10	Smoked Salmon and Cream Cheese Roll-Ups	Spinach and Walnut Stuffed Chicken Breast	Lemon Herb Grilled Salmon with Asparagus	Walnut and Dark Chocolate Energy Balls	Spinach and Blueberry Detox Smoothie
11	Avocado and Bacon Breakfast Skillet	Pork Stir-fry with Bell Peppers	Cilantro Lime Chicken with Avocado Salsa	Baked Asparagus Fries with Garlic Aioli	Tropical Coconut and Berry Blast
12	Sautéed Kale and Poached Eggs	Shrimp Avocado Salad with Lemon Dressing	Meatballs in Sugar-Free Marinara Sauce with Zucchini Spaghetti	Coconut Butter and Berry Fat Bombs	Cacao and Macadamia Nut Creamy Smoothie
13	Almond and Raspberry Breakfast Smoothie	Grilled Eggplant and Zucchini Stacks with Mozzarella	Spinach and Ricotta Stuffed Chicken Thighs	Almond and Herb Stuffed Olives	Avocado and Lime Digestive Smoothie
14	Chia Seed and Strawberry Breakfast Pudding	Greek Salad with Olives and Feta	Pesto Zucchini Noodles with Grilled Prawns	Cheese and Walnut Stuffed Bell Peppers	Chia and Berry Antioxidant Smoothie

Week 3

DAY	BREAKFAST	LUNCH	DINNER	SNACK	DESSERT
15	Cauliflower Hash Browns	Chard and Bacon Wrapped Scallops	Rosemary Lamb Stew with Turnips	Spicy Guacamole with Celery Sticks	Spinach, Cucumber, and Ginger Zing Smoothie
16	Sausage and Bell Pepper Breakfast Tacos (with Lettuce Wrap)	Cauliflower Fried Rice with Chicken	Spaghetti Squash Carbonara with Bacon	Pork Rind Nachos	Strawberry, Basil, and Coconut Fusion
17	Mixed Nut Granola with Coconut Milk	Beef and Vegetable Kebabs	Spinach and Ricotta Stuffed Peppers (Vegetarian)	Flaxseed and Parmesan Crackers	Creamy Vanilla and Mixed Nut Smoothie
18	Spinach and Feta Omelets	Grilled Chicken Caesar Salad with Kale and Homemade Dressing	Avocado and Strawberry Salad (Vegetarian)	Avocado and Tuna Salad Cups	Avocado and Spinach Green Smoothie
19	Coconut Yogurt with Mixed Berries	Broccoli and Cheddar Soup	Zucchini Lasagna with Spinach and Ricotta (Vegetarian)	Spinach and Feta Stuffed Mushrooms	Mixed Berry and Coconut Milk Smoothie
20	Kale and Avocado Scrambled Eggs	Spinach and Avocado Salad with Olive Oil Dressing	Broccoli and Cheddar Fritters (Vegetarian)	Baked Kale Chips with Sea Salt	Almond Butter and Chia Seed Smoothie
21	Zucchini Pancakes with Butter	Zucchini Noodle and Prawn Aglio Olio	Creamy Coconut and Vegetable Curry (Vegetarian)	Macadamia Nut Clusters with Dark Chocolate	Blueberry and Walnut Protein Smoothie

Week 4

DAY	BREAKFAST	LUNCH	DINNER	SNACK	DESSERT
22	Asparagus and Cheese Frittata	Asparagus and Goat Cheese Quiche	Stuffed Eggplant with Walnut and Cheese (Vegetarian)	Cucumber and Salmon Bite-sized Sandwiches	Strawberry and Cream Smoothie with Flaxseeds
23	Broccoli and Chicken Sausage Breakfast Casserole	Seared Tuna Salad with Mixed Greens	Asparagus and Goat Cheese Tart (Vegetarian)	Chia Seed and Coconut Milk Pudding	Chocolate and Avocado Keto Smoothie
24	Flaxseed Breakfast Porridge with Almond Milk	Lamb Kofta with Tzatziki Sauce	Chard and Feta Quiche (Vegetarian)	Zucchini and Parmesan Crisps	Cucumber and Mint Refreshing Smoothie
25	Coconut and Blueberry Muffins	Coconut Milk and Chicken Curry Soup	Mushroom and Spinach Stroganoff with Coconut Cream (Vegetarian)	Egg and Spinach Muffins	Raspberry and Coconut Cream Smoothie
26	Smoked Salmon and Cream Cheese Roll-Ups	Spinach and Walnut Stuffed Chicken Breast	Cauliflower and Cheese Gratin (Vegetarian)	Walnut and Dark Chocolate Energy Balls	Kale and Almond Smoothie with Lemon Zest
27	Avocado and Bacon Breakfast Skillet	Pork Stir-fry with Bell Peppers	Avocado and Almond Butter Toast on Flaxseed Bread (Vegetarian)	Baked Asparagus Fries with Garlic Aioli	Spinach and Blueberry Detox Smoothie
28	Sautéed Kale and Poached Eggs	Shrimp Avocado Salad with Lemon Dressing	Vegetable and Cheese Platter with Olive Tapenade (Vegetarian)	Coconut Butter and Berry Fat Bombs	Creamy Vanilla and Mixed Nut Smoothie

Conclusion

As we reach the culmination of this comprehensive guide, it's paramount to reflect on the significant lessons elucidated in *Super Easy Organic Low Carb Diet for Beginners*. The journey through the pages not only unveiled the science behind the low-carb approach but also emphasized the unparalleled benefits of organic foods. By integrating both these principles, this book has introduced readers to a wholesome, sustainable, and transformative way of eating.

Low-carb diets have garnered immense attention over the past years and for a good reason. As detailed in the first chapter, carbohydrates, especially refined ones, can have profound effects on insulin, a hormone deeply entwined with fat storage. By reducing carbohydrate intake, one can mitigate insulin spikes, enabling the body to utilize fat as an energy source more efficiently. This metabolic shift does more than just stimulate weight loss; it also offers stable energy, reduces cravings, and ensures better hormonal balance.

However, the importance of going low-carb doesn't overshadow the relevance of organic foods. Embracing an organic diet ensures that what we consume is devoid of harmful pesticides, synthetic hormones, and other toxins that can impair health and hinder weight loss goals. Organic foods, with their nutrient-dense profiles, not only support weight loss but also fortify overall well-being.

Setting oneself up for success, as articulated in the chapters, is not merely about understanding the principles. It requires a holistic approach – personalizing carb intake, leveraging technology for monitoring, and, most importantly, focusing on whole foods rather than getting lost in the maze of processed low-carb products available in the market. Whole foods, rich in fibers, natural fats, and nutrients, are pivotal for sustained weight management and overall health.

The exhaustive cookbook section offers a testament to the fact that adopting an organic, low-carb lifestyle does not mean compromising on taste or variety. From sumptuous breakfasts to savory dinners and even vegetarian options – there's something for everyone. The meticulous organization of the kitchen, budgeting tips, and dining-out strategies ensure that this lifestyle is not only nutritionally rewarding but also practically feasible.

As we conclude, it's essential to recognize that the core of this book is not about temporary dieting but adopting a lifestyle. It's about making informed, conscious choices that align with our health objectives and environmental consciousness. Whether you are someone just dipping your toes in the world of low-carb or a seasoned enthusiast, the emphasis on organic food highlights a path to a cleaner, healthier way of living.

In your hands, you hold more than just a guide; you possess a blueprint for a transformative journey. Weight loss, while a significant benefit, is just the tip of the iceberg. The real treasure lies in the enhanced vitality, clarity of mind, and profound satisfaction of knowing that you are consuming foods that are as good for the earth as they are for your body.

Embrace the principles, experiment with the recipes, and embark on a journey that promises holistic wellness. Remember, the journey to health is a marathon, not a sprint. Arm yourself with patience, stay committed, and let the organic low-carb way illuminate your path to optimum health.

Made in the USA
Monee, IL
15 March 2024

55102499R00063